Foreword by Steve Backlund

HOW HEAVEN INVADES YOUR FINANCES

JIM BAKER

How Heaven Invades Your Finances Book 1: Build the Foundation for Supernatural Finances
© Copyright 2015 by James Baker

This title is also available as an ebook through Amazon Kindle and Apple iBooks.

Requests for information should be addressed to: info@bakersequip.com

Cover Design: Robert Schwendenmann, bobbyhere.com
Interior Layout and Formatting: Robert Schwendenmann
Editors: Julie Mustard, Sally Schwendenmann

ISBN-10: 1505807662
ISBN-13: 978-1505807660

Build the Foundation for Supernatural Finances

TABLE OF CONTENTS

CONTENTS (continued)

DEDICATION

To **Mary Baker**:
A true worshipper in Spirit and truth.
You hold the key of David;
you're the best friend and wife I could ever imagine,
my constant encourager, balance-bringer, and fun-infuser.
Thank you for never being satisfied with less than more of Him.
You have made every step of this journey an absolute delight.
Thank you for making our home my favorite place on Earth.

And to the **Fabulous Baker Boys**:
You have brought me nothing but joy and honor…and endless laughter.
You are the type of friends every person dreams of.

Joshua—I love your warrior spirit and passion for justice; I love your compassion for the poor and your tenderness with kids. You have the heart of David's mighty men—willing to sacrifice all for the King. I love your integrity. You are a true prince in the Kingdom.

Wesley—You have the heart of David—extravagant worship for your extravagant King. You have your grandfather's kindness. I love your heart for relationships, the way you stick up for the hurting and wounded, and your passion to hear God's voice. You are a true Israelite in whom there is nothing false.

Evan—You have the heart of a giant-slayer. Nothing looks impossible to you because you see the size of your God. You are a creative genius, an adventurer, a leader, and the definition of "Awesome!" You are a burning one—you just can't help but shine.

AUTHOR'S NOTES

Since 2008, our church has seen some amazing breakthroughs in healing: deaf ears and blind eyes opened, creative miracles where missing body parts grew back, metal dissolved, six people raised from the dead, cancer healed, people got out of wheelchairs and more. Yea God! We pretty much went after healing with an all out ballistic assault.

In 2011, the Lord told me to go after breakthroughs in finances the way we went after breakthroughs in healing. I read over one hundred books that year and listened to numerous sermons. I meditated and prayed diligently over what I studied. In 2012, I did an eighteen-part sermon series called "When Heaven Invades Your Finances" (available at BakersEquip.ecwid.com). It shifted the mindsets of our church family and put us on a path for breakthrough. This book series is another step towards the pursuit of everything Jesus paid for.

This book has been life-changing for me to write. It is the product of learning from some of the best teachers on the planet and working it out in our family's life. I have given credit where credit is due to the best of my ability.

Out of all of the books I have read on finances, here are the ones I found the most helpful:

- *Wealth, Riches, & Money* by Craig Hill and Earl Pitts
- *Five Wealth Secrets 96% of Us Don't Know* by Craig Hill
- *Financial Stewardship* by Andrew Wommack
- *Money and the Prosperous Soul* by Stephen DeSilva
- *The Treasure Principle* by Randy Alcorn
- *Paid in Full* series by Roger Sapp
- *Hosting His Presence* by Bill Johnson
- *The Total Money Makeover* by Dave Ramsey
- *The Legacy Journey* by Dave Ramsey

ACKNOWLEDGMENTS

Thank you, **Steve Backlund**, for encouraging this book, for letting me be a part of your writing team on *Help! I'm a Pastor*, and for "making" me have a deadline for this book to be completed. I love the way you lead through fathering. Thank you for granting permission to use some of your declarations.

Thank you **Zion Christian Fellowship**, the most dangerous group of believers alive today: thank you for your encouragement, prayers, risks, acceptance, hunger, perseverance, honor, and contending with us to see a region transformed. You are our heart and joy.

Thank you to the "**Zioneers**" who wrote testimonies for the "Heaven Invading" sections of this book. May your breakthroughs become a catalyst for heaven invading the finances of others.

To my friends who read a draft of this book and gave input: **Sierra "The Golden Wordsmith" Clouse, Sean "Kal-El" O'Rourke, Josh "Firestorm" Lawrence, Cheryl Baker (Mom), Eddie "XP" Jewell, Ciara "The Chameleon" Lewis, Channing "Chi-Chi" Lawrence,** and **David "The one known as 'The Prophet'" Jonas.**

To the **elders** of Zion Christian Fellowship, thank you for linking arms with us, for holding up our arms, for keeping His voice and Presence the main thing, for navigating uncharted waters with a steady hand and wisdom—you are some of my heroes: (our current elders) **Kevin Costello, Sam Costello, Mark Land, Mark Tomallo,** (previous elders) **Chuck Warner,** and **Bill Johnston.**

Thank you **Bill Johnson, Craig Hill,** and **Stephen DeSilva** for granting permission for the use of parts of your material; but more than that, for your influence on my life.

Thank you to my pastor, **Cleddie Keith**, for being the hungriest man I know, for never changing the subject, for your continual encouragement and wisdom, and for being a father to so many. When I think of you, I know "there were giants in the earth in those days."

I want to thank **Julie Mustard** for her editing genius and for moving this book forward by having my sermon series transcribed for me. You are awesome! Thank you **Robert Schwendenmann** for the perfect book cover and the layout and design of the interior. I love your spirit of excellence! Thank you to the **Bethel interns** who transcribed the sermon series that turned into this book.

My prayer is that as you study this book, you will have the encounter that God desires for you to have so that you can become the witness this world desperately needs you to be: a beloved child who is well taken care of by their heavenly Father.

ENDORSEMENTS

What a phenomenal subject: *How Heaven Invades Your Finances*. Jim Baker has a vision for the invasion of the supernatural into every area of our natural.

Many believe Heaven can invade our hearts and forgive our sins. It doesn't seem difficult to accept Heaven invading our broken relationships with restoration. We are thrilled with Heaven's healing invading Earth's diseases. But mention the power of Heaven invading our finances and ears deafen, minds close, and religion raises its pious head with accusation and confusion. Heaven is not selective in its invasion. It desires to free us in every area of our lives.

While the love of money in our hearts is the root of all evil, the lack of money in our hands is often the root of broken homes, shattered dreams and inability to help others.

While there has been false teaching concerning Kingdom Finances, there has also been false teaching on grace, faith, hope, etc. The existence of counterfeit teaching does not make void the truth. Rather, it authenticates it.

As you walk with Jim Baker on this revelation journey of *How Heaven Invades Your Finances*, religious tradition and trendy heresy will fall away and the blockages clogging God's provision pipeline can be eliminated.

Dr. Mike Brown
Strength and Wisdom Ministries

Pastor Jim Baker sheds much needed revelatory light on the critical questions that have long concerned many over finances and what the Bible teaches. His book is both inspirational as well as educational. This book will open your eyes and your heart to see the wonderful aspects of Father's heart to provide for His children. I recommend this book to all; you will be blessed and challenged to take a new bold stand in living and giving for the glory of God.

Bobby Conner
Eagles View Ministries

How Heaven Invades Your Finances is a wonderful, profound and incredible book that I would encourage everybody to read. It's practical, insightful, full of truth and loaded with Kingdom. I know this book will renew your mindset into thinking about money from another perspective, which is God's value system. It has the ability to set you free from poverty and bring you into the generosity mindset of God's Kingdom. Jim has not just written this from an informational perspective; I know that he walks out and practices what he teaches.

Chris Gore
Director Healing Ministries, Bethel Church
Author of *Walking in Supernatural Healing Power*

Today, too many of God's people are "weary and heavy laden" with financial teaching aimed primarily at gaining access to their bank accounts. They also often feel overwhelmed with pressure to do more with less. But, what if they could do more with… MORE?

As one who knows Jim Baker's teaching on finances I can promise you that this book will be a breath of fresh air to you and to anyone wise enough to venture into it's pages. You will be filled with confidence instead of condemnation as you learn to reject poverty mindsets and begin to realize your Kingdom potential.

How Heaven Invades Your Finances will revolutionize your thinking and bring the joy of heaven into your daily financial decisions. Let the invasion begin!!

Timothy M. Hacker
Senior Pastor – Harvest Life Fellowship
Author of *GOTNOPHOBIA: Progressive, Contagious and Incurable Courage*

In this book, Jim sets aright much of the biblical misinformation regarding personal financial management that many people have believed all their lives. You may be very **surprised to find out what Jesus actually said about money** and how He encourages His followers to manage finances. I have found that actual truth is like a pure, clear river, but there are also stagnant, muddy backwaters on either side of the river. Many people don't realize that they have gotten stuck in the mud on one bank or the other until someone exposes the muddy water and helps them see where the clear channel of the river is. That is exactly what Jim has masterfully done in this book regarding our attitude toward, and management of, money.

As you read this book, you will discover how to get out of the stagnant, muddy backwaters, and right into the main river channel of God's supernatural financial abundance. Whether you have a lot of money or little money, if you want to **learn to live and manage finances in God's supernatural power and wisdom**, then this book is for you.

Craig Hill
Founder of Family Foundations International www.familyfoundations.com
Author of several books and a seminar on Biblical financial management

May God be gracious to us and bless us and make His face to shine upon us, that Your way may be known on earth, Your saving power among all nations (Psalm 67:1-2).

For most of the years that I have walked with the Father, this prayer has been one of the deep cries of my heart. As I travel around the world, I encounter fellow believers whom Holy Spirit is stirring with the same cry. The world is waiting to see a people who carry the promised blessing of the Lord as a visible sign of His goodness. I believe with everything in me that He is longing to pour it out upon His people exceedingly more than we long to receive it!

Jim Baker has tapped into the Father's heart in this matter and written a book that will help us begin to move in that direction. Revelation about walking in the blessing is flowing from Heaven to Earth, and if you will meditate on the truths contained in these pages, that revelation will begin to land on you. I have had the honor of calling Jim Baker my friend for several years and I believe in him. We have not yet learned to walk in our full inheritance, but anointed leaders like Jim Baker are helping us to get there. Heaven is invading the Earth!

David Jonas
International Speaker and Catalyst

I find it interesting that the word "steward" comes from the story of an ancient king who was seeking to find the most disciplined and frugal servant in his kingdom. His intention was to place him over all the kingdom's finances. The one who was chosen was the "Keeper of the Sty," which is an enclosure for swine or pigs. An ancient root for the word steward is: *styward/stigward*. This book takes a refreshing and practical approach to financial freedom. It is a book whose time, like the author's, has come. It is as if God has given him fresh eyes to help others see Kingdom finance more clearly. His style of writing is prayer-soaked and filled with profound truth which has a mental jolt to it.

Cleddie Keith
Senior Pastor Heritage Fellowship, Florence, KY

When Jim Baker speaks, I listen. I do this for two reasons. First, because he is one of the few believers I know who functions both with a marketplace anointing and a Pastoral mantle. He understands both worlds. Second, Jim is a bonafide worker of miracles, and that is a rarity in itself. You cannot help but profit from hearing what he has to say. I always do.

Lance Wallnau
The Lance Learning Group

FOREWORD

When I heard about Jim Baker's eighteen-part sermon series on finances (and that he read over 100 books preparing for those messages), I immediately thought to myself, "He has tapped into truths the body of Christ must hear."

Jim never does anything halfway. Whether in family life or a spiritual revelation like healing, he has the unique ability and passion to go up to the headwaters concerning those things. Those who get into his world have the great privilege of benefiting from what he finds. It is virtually impossible to stay mediocre when you are around him.

I have had the privilege of knowing Jim for many years. I have spoken at his church numerous times, and I have found he is one of the most insightful leaders I know. Because of this, I asked him to assist me in writing *Help! I Am a Pastor*, a book of practical wisdom for church leaders. Jim has become a good friend and important part of my ministry emphasis.

In *How Heaven Invades Your Finances*, Jim Baker mixes humor with life-changing truths in a way that everyone can relate to. He uses his personal life lessons as an example of how he has learned that we are not in charge of our finances, but God is. He emphasizes good stewardship and making wise financial decisions, but this book goes way beyond those things by infusing the reader with keys to bring heaven to earth in this most important area of life – our money.

Get ready for new intimacy with Daddy God. Get ready for impactful revelation. Get ready for blessing. Get ready to laugh. Get ready to have some of your doctrinal sacred cows killed. Get ready to see financial worry dismantled. Get ready to become an increased financier of Kingdom advancement in the days ahead. I declare you will never be the same again after reading this book.

Steve Backlund
Founder of Igniting Hope Ministries

"No one would have remembered the Good Samaritan if he'd only had good intentions. He had money as well."

- Margaret Thatcher

Heaven Invading: The House Swap

Growing up, I was always taught not to go into debt. When I became a Christian, I learned that God did not want us to be in debt either. So, how were we going to buy our first house—debt free?

We made a plan and were able to buy a modest house without any debt! As we became more involved in our church, we wanted to move closer to be a part of the work there.

One day the thought occurred to me, "Well, just trade your house." I had heard of people trading cars, but never houses. I spoke with a Christian friend of mine who is a realtor. "Where did you get that thought?" he asked. "I don't even know how that could work." "I think God told me," I replied.

After that, I found a broken down wreck of a house and was convinced the owners would gladly trade with me since our home was much nicer. Clearly, my faith wasn't very high.

My wife drew out a floor plan of what she needed: a kitchen, dining room, an open floor plan so she could see the kids playing and space to homeschool them. As we were "shopping" for houses, we walked into a particular house that had the exact floor plan that Anne had drawn out. We didn't know about prophetic drawing, but it worked! We began to "claim" that this was the house for us.

Interestingly, a construction worker from our church was riding in a van with seven of his co-workers—one of them just happened to own the house we wanted. He said, "I don't know what is going to happen, but I think I am going to have to move because this guy is claiming my house. I don't want to move, but my wife wants to, so I guess I am going to have to move out of my house."

My faith soared when I heard that story. Two months later, a moving van showed up at my house and his house—and we swapped homes! This new house was a major upgrade for us in house-size and lot-size—with no money out of pocket. We moved from an 1800 square-foot house on a half-acre lot and traded for a 3000 square foot house on three acres with its own lake, a brand new three-car garage, and a beautiful cement basketball court off the back.

What God will do for me, He will do for you. What He will do for you, He will do for me. He is a good Dad.

Kevin and Anne

CHAPTER 1

Prosperity Isn't Optional

Back in the late 1990's, I was an associate pastor at a church in Winston-Salem, NC. One of the members of the church was an executive for a mattress company. He told my wife and me that he could get us a huge discount on their best mattress, which was a huge blessing, since the mattress we had was so old that it felt like we were sleeping on a pile of unfolded laundry. The only catch was that I had to drive forty-five minutes to Greensboro to pick the mattress up directly from the factory.

I get lost easily...even with GPS, so this journey was more than interesting. I made the forty-five minute drive in our mini-van, mostly freeway driving, and arrived at the factory in time to pick up our new mattress. As I walked into the warehouse, I was greeted by a factory worker who didn't look like he was filled with "joy unspeakable." With no expression on his face he said, "Are you Baker? I'll help you put the mattress on your vehicle."

Together we lugged the queen-size, pillow-top mattress across the warehouse and placed it on top of our minivan. He handed me some rope and scissors and walked away. I realized at this point that he is leaving me solely responsible for securing this mattress to the roof of my van so that it doesn't fly onto the freeway at 65+ mph and create a ten-car pile up. My sweat glands immediately activated, and I quickly began praying and fasting. I wrapped the rope around the mattress several times, making a series of intricate loops–front to back, side to side. I think I even invented a new knot. It looked good—Eagle Scout good. Feeling confident and like I deserved a merit badge, I drove the 65 mph speed limit home.

Knowing I would need help once I got home, a friend was waiting at my house to help me unload the mattress and bring it into our bedroom. With a horrified look on his face, he asked, "What have you done? How did you make it home?"

I was confused, "What are you talking about?"

"The mattress is not tied to anything. You literally tied the mattress to itself. Look…" and he slid the mattress right off of the roof without untying a single knot. Now, I don't know if God sent a fat angel to sit on it during the drive home or woke up some intercessors in China to pray for me, but it was a miracle that it made it ten feet, not to mention 40 miles.

I tell this story as a parable for how many Christians are living their financial lives: **they want to carry this giant blessing into their house, but they haven't given God anything to attach it to.** This book is about giving God something to attach His blessing to by laying the foundation for supernatural finances.

WHAT IS "PROSPERITY"?

Mary (my wife) and I know a Christian couple that has a 10,000 square foot house decorated by an interior designer, a huge swimming pool, who drive luxury cars and boats, and who enjoy expensive vacations. They were both working excessive hours to pay for this extravagant lifestyle. A friend of mine was talking to them about giving and generosity and they replied, "We can't afford to give right now." Let me ask you, "Is this couple prosperous?"

"Real prosperity is defined by how much we give away, not by how much we keep for ourselves."

One of the biggest problems that people immediately have with any teaching on prosperity comes from the belief that *prosperity is selfish.* Newsflash: ***Prosperity is not selfish. Prosperity is not all about you.*** For the Christian, the motivation for prosperity is about desiring to have the resources to bless others and accomplish what God has called you to do. It is not about indulging every greed or desire.

Andrew Wommack says, "Real prosperity is defined by how much we give away, not by how much we keep for ourselves."[1] Prosperity is about blessing, not possessing.

And God is able to make __all__ grace __abound__ to you, so that having __all__ sufficiency in __all__ things at __all__ times, you may __abound__ in __every__ good work (2 Corinthians 9:8).

True prosperity is having more than enough so that you can "abound in every good work." If this verse isn't true, then John 3:16 isn't true either. Go back and read the underlined words.

Dr. Mike Brown's definition of "financial authority" highlights the fact that prosperity is not an end of itself, but a means of serving others:

God not only desires to deliver you from financial bondage [debt] but to position you into financial authority to where you are empowered to fulfill every divine assignment and help others fulfill theirs.[2]

Prosperity doesn't mean that every Christian is going to be a millionaire. It does imply, however, that we should have finances proportionate to our assignments from the Lord and more than enough to be a blessing to others. True prosperity is God-centered, not man-centered.

If you think of yourself as a conduit or a hose through which God's blessings can flow, then it makes sense that the inside of a hose would get wet! Prosperity is about giving. When you get that attitude, God will get money to you—and there will be plenty left over for you. If God can get money through you, He can get money to you. When the priority of your finances is on God rather than yourself, God will take better care of you on "accident" than you ever could on purpose. Remember, His name is *El Shaddai*, not *El Cheapo*.[3]

Has there been abuse by people teaching on prosperity in the past? Yes. There has also been false teaching on heaven, but I am still planning on going there. Many have taught prosperity from a selfish standpoint, as if it is all about getting more and "having it all." You aren't going to see a supernatural return on your giving when you do it with the wrong motive. God is more concerned with the motive behind the action than the action itself. Giving with a wrong heart is of no benefit—it's just attempted bribery.

This book will deal with the heart issues. We must develop the right

"The whole purpose of money is to drive you into greater intimacy with God."

motivation behind financial stewardship on purpose because it doesn't come naturally to many people. I've heard Dallas Willard say, "The biggest hindrance to experiencing God's Kingdom is my kingdom."

A lot of people just want principles for financial increase, "Show me what to do. How much do I need to give? Teach me about the seed. What are the laws, the principles of the Kingdom?" A person fixated on principles without the Prince keeps a person under the Law trying to do their best to obey God's without God's help.[4] Good luck with that! All of the principles of Scripture assume a life that is intimately connected to and empowered by the Prince. Kingdom without the King is the basis of witchcraft.

The whole purpose of money is to drive you into greater intimacy with God. If you have wealth, you will need the revelation and strategy of what God wants you to do with that wealth. If you are building wealth, you will need the revelation and strategy of what God wants you to do with what you do have. All of life flows out of intimacy with God.

BEING BLESSED IS REQUIRED [5]

When God only provides for your needs, the earth is lacking the revelation of an abundant Father.

> *May God be gracious to us and bless us and make His face to shine upon us, that Your way may be known on earth, Your saving power among all nations* (Psalm 67:1-2).

That sounds like revival to me. People lack a knowledge of the goodness of God. Our attitude needs to be, "Put Your hand on my life so they see what You're like." Look at the verses above again. It is saying, "They won't know what You're like unless they see Your blessing and favor on me."

One of the most underrated tools for ministering to this world is having a blessed life. The face of the Lord "shining" upon you reveals His ways to a world in great need. If you have ever seen a grandparent looking at their grandchild with joy and delight, you have seen a face "shining." The best testimony to the world is the favor of God that is on your life.

So even though wisdom is better than strength, those who are wise will be despised if they are poor. What they say will not be appreciated for long (Ecclesiastes 9:16 NLT).

If you are a businessman, don't expect to have a great impact unless you prosper financially. Prosper so that you can be a father or mother to others in business. Prosper that you can have Kingdom dominion—which means you come low to serve and empower others to succeed.

You may be asking, "Jim, isn't all this talk of prosperity just a 'bless me' club?" Well, would you rather be a part of a "curse me" club? Exactly, what is the problem with a "bless me" club? Christians just give away more the more they get. We recognize that we are blessed to be a blessing. In order to be a blessing...wait for it...you need to first be blessed! One of the most self-centered, destructive attitudes in the church is to not seek a blessing. This makes us ill-equipped to re-present what Dad is like.

Jesus Christ's life, death, burial, resurrection, and ascension have made those who turn to Him the very children of God. We become "heirs of God" (Romans 8:17)—we get to inherit God! It doesn't get any more prosperous than that. And as His child you are eternally, beautifully, and blissfully blessed (Ephesians 1:3). It's chronic. You are stuck in this. Some may call it a "bless me" club; Jesus calls it "abundant life" (John 10:10).

Think of it this way: **you are obligated to be blessed**—goodness and mercy are tracking you down and stalking you every day (Psalm 23:6). You owe it to the people around you. I am not talking about building your own empire. I am not talking about the attitude of, "I'm rich. You're not." You can be rich and not be blessed; blessing is never measured by dollars—that is a byproduct. It is measured in favor, open doors, wisdom, and strategies. You can't take credit for blessing because you didn't do it. The world needs to see a people for whom life works—they enjoy their family, are generous, have joy in the midst of problems, and peace in the midst of storms.

Part of that means learning to enjoy the material world God created without falling in love with it (1 Timothy 6:17). That doesn't mean a life without problems. None of us can live without conflict and difficulty; the difference is what we do when it comes our way. Joseph was promoted to the head of the prison. God's blessing didn't wipe out the prison sentence; however, it did cause him to be elevated in the environment he was assigned to. It is the hand of the Lord upon you that will capture the attention of

"God intended for each succeeding generation to excel beyond the past generation in every area of life."

others. Is it possible that the greatest revival will come when God's favor and blessing come upon His children so indisputably and evidently that what people see will draw them to God?

But seek first the Kingdom of God and His righteousness, and all these things will be added to you (Matthew 6:33).

We like the guy who seeks first the Kingdom. And then religion questions him when the "all these things" are added to him, even though that's a part of the promise!

Humble yourselves, therefore, under the mighty hand of God so that at the proper time He may exalt you (1 Peter 5:6).

We like the guy who humbles himself. Some aren't too sure about him when God exalts him. You never need to apologize for the blessing of the Lord. You do need His wisdom and grace to walk in it.

Do you want to be a "good man"? "A good man leaves an inheritance to his children's children" (Proverbs 13:22). God intended for each succeeding generation to excel beyond the past generation in every area of life. There has to be a level of blessing from the Lord and effective stewardship on our end in order to leave behind an inheritance for two generations.[6]

The Lord has designed life in such a way that by living under the blessing of the Lord, we manifest His nature to a world that is ignorant about what He is like. It's simple but, if we get it, we will change generations and nations.

INNER ACTION

Take a few minutes to engage in an exercise of ruthlessly honest observation concerning your heart and prosperity.[7] The purpose of this exercise is to help you see reality. This is not a time to criticize yourself through self-judgment, "I shouldn't feel this way" or "I shouldn't think that." Stay objective through the process.

1. It's a bold statement: "You are obligated to be blessed." What kind of thoughts or feelings are triggered when you think about "financial prosperity":

Delight	Dissatisfaction	Envy
Disappointment	Anxiety	Excitement
Insecurity	Peace of mind	Gratitude
Contentment	Guilt	Trust
Greed	Anger	Regret

2. How has unbalanced teaching on the "Prosperity Gospel" influenced your thinking on the subject? Does it make it difficult to hear that word without cringing?

3. Ask God the following questions and wait quietly for Him to respond. Write down any pictures or impressions you receive.

"God, what lies am I believing about my finances?"
"God, what is the truth You want to give me in exchange?"

4. Take a few moments to reflect on your upbringing. How would you summarize the story of your family's life concerning money, possessions, and teaching on prosperity as you were growing up? What perspectives on money did you catch from your parents' attitudes and behaviors - positive or negative?

5. What do you want to see happen in your life as you study this book? Give God an open invitation to do His work in your life.

Additional Resource

Keys to Heaven's Economy by Shawn Bolz

Endnotes

1. Andrew Wommack, *Financial Stewardship* (Tulsa, OK: Harrison House, 2012), 105.

2. Dr. Mike Brown in a message called "Financial Authority" available at www. StrengthandWisdomMinistries.com. This is one of the best messages I have ever heard on finances. After listening to it in the car on a road trip with my kids, they said, "Dad, we have to bring him to Zion!" (Our church).

3. "El Shaddai" is one of the Hebrew names of God in the Old Testament and is often translated as "God Almighty."

4. "Law" or "religion" is dedicating oneself to the keeping of rules, rituals and formulas by which you can come to God. The reason for the devotion and the dedication is to please God and to be accepted by Him. It is based on performance. "Grace" recognizes that Jesus paid for it all, so there is nothing left for us to earn. We learn to receive by faith. In *How Heaven Invades Your Finances Book 2: Revolutionize Your Living, Giving & Receiving,* we will look at what giving looks like under grace, since God is not dealing with us based on our performance.

5. Most of what follows in this section is from notes I took from a message Bill Johnson gave at Bethel Cleveland Church in October 2011. Used with permission. Bill also has an excellent message called "Being Blessed is Required" that addresses this topic available at https://shop.ibethel.org/products/open-heavens-october-2010-complete-set.

6. Craig Hill has the most amazing testimony and plan for this in his book, *Five Wealth Secrets 96% of Us Don't Know* (Littleton, CO: Family Foundations International, 2012).

7. Adapted from an exercise from *Giving: Unlocking the Heart of Good Stewardship* by John Ortberg, Laurie Pederson, and Judson Poling (Grand Rapids: Zondervan, 2000), 20.

Heaven Invading: Jobs and Better Jobs

Whenever my husband had a bad day at work, he would stop at the store and buy us something. He said that surprising us with gifts made it all worth it. He just loves to give gifts.

He was an executive at a company. One day, as he was reviewing some company financial papers, he saw some reoccurring discrepancies.

He brought the discrepancies to the attention of the president of the company assuming it was just a mistake. After seeing the president's reaction to his findings, he realized it was not just a mistake. Soon after their conversation, my husband went overseas on a short-term business trip.

When he returned, his boss had given his office to someone else and started excluding him from all meetings. When he came home that day he brought bags of gifts. He bought an entire outfit for our daughter and a China tea set for me that I had once admired. He said nothing about what had transpired at the office. He put the whole situation in the Lord's hands, knowing He would supply.

We had just begun building a house and were planning our daughter's wedding. He did not know how long he would have a job, so he started updating his résumé.

Before the résumés were in the mail, he received a call from a headhunter who was referred to my husband regarding a particular job opportunity. He interviewed and got the job for more money with a signing bonus that paid for our daughter's wedding.

Jim and Cheryl (Dad and Mom)

CHAPTER 2

The Kindergarten of the Spiritual Life

have a confession to make: I like to watch blooper TV shows. What's not to love about them? There's one sports blooper episode that really stands out in my mind. In it, a guy who has never snow-skied before has somehow been convinced by his friends to ski down a slope with a vertical ramp while they video-record the ordeal.

This particular ramp happens to be designed for the Olympic event called "aerial skiing." In that event, the aerialist skier speeds down the hill and launches off a six-to-twelve foot jump, which propels him or her up to sixty feet above the landing. Once in the air, the aerialist performs multiple flips and twists before touching down on an inclined landing hill.

Beofre attempting this feat, this man's "friends," running on sizeable amounts of alcohol and testosterone, try to fill him with icy courage and steely resolve by declaring this over his life: "Go big or go home!" This phrase resonates with this man so much that he keeps chanting it. It doesn't matter that he has never skied before. It doesn't matter that he is going to be plummeting head first towards the earth from fifty feet in the air. "Go big or go home!"

Before you know it, he is at the top of the ski slope, chanting his mantra one last time before plunging over the edge of the ramp. The video camera follows him as he races down the hill at full speed, soars off of the ramp like a phoenix rising on the horizon, reaches forty to fifty feet in the air, and... can you picture it? Did he go big or go home? Well, he did both. He went big and he went home...in a body cast. He landed on his head.

Remarkably, the episode continues, following the man to the hospital, where his "friends" are now filming him *in traction*. It turns out that he has broken almost every bone in his body. The doctors say it is a miracle he is alive, and that he will recover and walk someday. From his hospital bed, he retells his story of valor and then gazes into the camera to recite his newfound words of wisdom one more time, as if to justify his actions: "Go big or go home."

It seems that the "hero" of this video learned a lesson the hard way: *if you can't do that which is least, you can't do that which is greater.* If you can't ski, you shouldn't be going on Olympic vertical ramps. If you can't run to the fridge during TV commercials without getting winded, you can't run a marathon. If you can't do a push-up, you shouldn't try to bench press 500 pounds.

We understand this principle in the natural, but in the spiritual realm we violate this all of the time. In Luke 16, Jesus has just told the parable of the unjust steward; this guy was wasting his master's resources he was in charge of and he gets caught. He does some dishonest things to secure his future and Jesus says these words:

> *He who is faithful in what is <u>least</u> is faithful also in much; and he who is unjust in what is least is unjust also in much* (Luke 16:10 NKJV).

It is interesting that Jesus called money that which "is least." He went on to say:

> *And if you are untrustworthy about worldly wealth, who will trust you with the true riches of heaven* (Luke 16:11 NLT)?

Jesus said in this parable that trusting God in the area of finances is

---

"Money is the kindergarten of the spiritual life."

---

the *least area* of trusting God. It is the least use of faith, and you can't do greater things without doing the lesser things first.[1] Most Christians don't believe this is true. Most Christians think it is easier for them to have faith for their loved ones to get saved, or for physical healing, or for a new job. Most Christians feel like trusting God for money is the hardest thing to believe for. For them, it's not the least—it's the greatest, especially since it causes them the greatest amount of stress and anxiety.

Let's put it this way: money is the kindergarten of the spiritual life. So anything that you want to see in your life that you would consider "more," you have to do that which is "least" first. If you can't jump two feet, you can't jump across the Grand Canyon. If you can't pick up a football, you can't throw it fifty yards.

Do you remember when the big "Y2K" scare was being hyped up? The fear was inspired around the idea that all of our computer systems would fail on January 1, 2000 because most computers would not be able to distinguish between the year 2000 and 1900. In the wake of this earth-shattering glitch, we would be forced to live without electricity, running water, heat, etc. Of course nothing ever happened, but it got a lot of press leading up to it.

I remember there was one guy at our church that really bought into the "Millennial Bug." He taught classes at his house on how to prepare for the coming disaster. He even bought medicine made for horses in full belief that it was cheaper to stock it up and use his conversion charts to adjust the dosage for human consumption. He converted his cash into ammunition fully convinced that it would be the new currency.

But for some reason, he didn't stock up on any food or water. I thought this was particularly strange since he believed that civilized society was on the verge of collapse. Maybe he thought we would revert back to being hunters/gatherers? Nope.

When I asked him what he planned on doing for food if there was a crisis, he immediately replied, "God will have the ravens feed me like he did Elijah." As our conversation continued, he brought up the subject of giving to the church and he explained how he didn't believe in tithing. He claimed that he couldn't afford to give 10% and currently didn't give anything. As we talked more, he shared that "tithing didn't work" and how he was afraid that if he gave, he wouldn't have enough for himself. Listen: if you do not have the faith to give God any of your income during a time of prosperity, you won't have the faith for ravens to feed you during a crisis.

There are so many people waking up to their identity in Christ and dreaming with God about their destiny, but they are trying to bypass this issue and move on to bigger things. It won't work. Just like other areas of your life, you must start at the beginning and work your way up. You can't jump from the ground to the top of a twenty-foot ladder. You have to start on the bottom rung and work your way up. Trusting God with your finances is the bottom rung of the ladder. It's the starting place.[2]

Here is some good news: the reverse is also true. If you *can* be trusted with money, then you *can* be trusted with true riches—and true riches are more than just money.

TRUE RICHES

What are the "true riches"? The apostle Paul tells us in Colossians 2:2-3 that it is in Christ Himself "are hidden all the treasures of wisdom and knowledge." Jesus is the ultimate Prize. He is the pearl of great price and the treasure hidden in a field that is worth selling everything to gain.[3] Christ Himself is the treasure that we seek—not money. When you have Jesus, you have access to everything He had access to.[4]

Here's a chart comparing earthly riches with true riches:

Earthly Riches	True Riches
Buy someone a meal	Multiply one meal to feed thousands[5]
Pay your hospital bill	Empty out a hospital
Give flowers at a funeral	Wreck the funeral by raising the dead[6]
Buy a hearing aid	Reattach someone's severed-off ear[7]
A budget	Abundance[8]
Presents	Presence[9]
Give to the poor	Eliminate poverty in a city[10]
I succeed	Empowering others to succeed

The goal is not "How much can I get?" The goal is "How much can I give and be a blessing?"

True riches are not about having more money. It has nothing to do with money; however, the way you handle the money God gives you will determine how much of true riches you are entrusted with. The goal is not "How much can I get?" The goal is "How much can I give and be a blessing?" Jesus spells this out in another parable:[11]

> *The crowd was listening to everything Jesus said. And because He was nearing Jerusalem, He told them a story to correct the impression that the Kingdom of God would begin right away* (Luke 19:11 NLT).

The crowd thought the Kingdom of God would appear immediately. They did not understand how the Kingdom would come. They had an appetite, so Jesus tells this story to satisfy it.

> He said, "A nobleman was called away to a distant empire to be crowned king and then return" (Luke 19:12 NLT).

Jesus is the nobleman in this story. He will leave the Earth to receive His Kingdom and then return to Earth on the Father's specified day.

> Before he left, he called together ten of his servants and divided among them ten pounds of silver, saying, "Invest this for me while I am gone." But his people hated him and sent a delegation after him to say, "We do not want him to be our king."
> After he was crowned king, he returned and called in the servants to whom he had given the money. He wanted to find out what their profits were. The first servant reported, "Master, I invested your money and made ten times the original amount!"
> "Well done!" the king exclaimed. "You are a good servant. You have been faithful with the little I entrusted to you, so you will be governor of ten cities as your reward."
> The next servant reported, "Master, I invested your money and made five times the original amount."
> "Well done!" the king said. "You will be governor over five cities."
> But the third servant brought back only the original amount of money and said, "Master, I hid your money and kept it safe. I was afraid because you are a hard man to deal with, taking what isn't yours and harvesting crops you didn't plant."
> "You wicked servant!" the king roared. "Your own words condemn you. If you knew that I'm a hard man who takes what isn't mine and harvests crops I didn't plant, why didn't you deposit my money in the bank? At least I could have gotten some interest on it"
> (Luke 19:13-23 NLT).

This third servant had a wrong view of the king, making him fearful and disobedient. He didn't realize the king gave him something to steward so that he could reward him and increase his influence. His view of the king was distorted and, as a result, he actually accused the king of being harsh and unfair.

Dallas Willard says, "All human troubles come from thinking of God wrongly." [12] There are many people who do not see God properly and therefore do not experience who He really is. In the Kingdom, you don't get what you need; you get what you believe that is in alignment with His truth. To the extent that you believe the true nature of God is the extent you will truly experience Him in your life (2 Peter 1:3).

Your mind is like the valve that determines the flow of abundant life from heaven. If you think God is harsh, judgmental, and crabby, then the goodness of God will not flow into your life the way He wants because that is not what you have faith for. Unfortunately, some may reap the fruit of their own negative perception and attitudes rather than the goodness and grace of God in Jesus.

> *Then, turning to the others standing nearby, the king ordered, "Take the money from this servant, and give it to the one who has ten pounds."*
>
> *"But, master," they said, "he already has ten pounds!"*
>
> *"Yes," the king replied, "and to those who use well what they are given, even more will be given. But from those who do nothing, even what little they have will be taken away"* (Luke 19:24-26 NLT).

And so the one who wasn't faithful had his taken and it was given to the one who now has the most. It looks like Jesus is not a socialist. [13] Jesus always rewards faithfulness with additional resources. Someone wrote to Bill Johnson, "The rich keep getting richer." He responded:

> *True: revelation handled well attracts revelation, mercy given to others well attracts more mercy, proper stewardship of resources attracts more resources. This is the kingdom. What we do with what God gives us is the test.* [14]

HOW THE KINGDOM COMES

Do you remember why Jesus was giving this parable? [15] He was telling them this story to show that the Kingdom was not going to show up the way they thought.

> *The crowd was listening to everything Jesus said. And because He was nearing Jerusalem, He told them a story to correct the impression that*

the Kingdom of God would begin right away (Luke 19:11 NLT).

We keep expecting the Kingdom to flow out of heaven instead of flowing through us. Many Christians are waiting for revival to strike or the glory cloud to settle over a region and zap people; they think that is how the Kingdom will come. Jesus revealed to His followers that the Kingdom comes through stewardship and the key to shaping the culture over cities is stewarding what you have in your pocket.

Let's make the story simpler. Jesus says, "So, you want to know how the Kingdom of God is going to come to Earth? It's like a king who gives a guy ten $100 bills. The guy stewards the money, invests it, and brings back twenty $100 bills. The king is pleased and rewards him, 'You are now governor. You are in charge of ten cities.'"

Do you want to touch cities? Jesus hid the key in this parable. By giving His servants money to handle, the King is looking to find those who can rule faithfully with Him in His Kingdom. The reward for faithfulness is to share in the King's authority, to be part of the family business. Ruling in the Kingdom is always the empowerment to serve more effectively, not a power play.[16]

I don't know what that does to you, but it makes something inside me want to explode! It makes me cry out to God, "Help me get this money thing right so that I can influence cities to be 'on earth as it is in heaven'!"

Here's the other side of that reality. If we don't get our hearts right toward money, we can blow the shofar, Jericho-march around the city seven times, make declarations, fast, pray, but if you cannot do that which is least, you cannot do that which is greater.

What is it that you want to see God do in and through you? What is your dream?

- Entire cities saved?
- A nation saved in a day?
- Hospitals cleared out?
- Down syndrome healed regularly?
- End human trafficking in your state?
- Elimination of abortion?
- Economies of the poorest nations turned around?
- Literacy in the inner city?

- No more poverty in your city?
- Your city to be a "divorce-free" zone?
- Give away $1 Million?
- Plant churches?
- World missions?
- The Kingdom of God to invade the seven mind-molders of society? [17]

"Your destiny will always level off at the level of your financial stewardship."

A tennis player trains by practicing tennis. A singer trains by singing. A leader trains by leading. Our stewardship over the finances entrusted to us is "Training for Reigning." Our learning to "reign with Christ" and co-labor with Him to bring heaven to earth starts with how we handle the money in our hand.

I don't care how many prophetic words you've received, how many angelic encounters you've had, how many healings you've seen, how many people think that you are an apostle, what title you have in front of your name, how much money you have in your bank account...if you are not faithful with that which is least, you cannot do that which is greater. Your destiny will always level off at the level of your financial stewardship.

God passionately desires to reward faithful stewards with the influence to shape the culture over cities. It all starts with how you manage what you have right now. Kris Vallotton echoes this cry of the Father:

> We are in the midst of the greatest revival in human history. Yet there remains a distance between what should be and what will be. That distance is you! What will you be? You are the bridge between history and His story. You are the sons of the prophets! The sick, the demonized, the poor, the blind, the lame, and the lost are waiting to see what you have learned. Don't disappoint them! [18]

When it comes to how we approach the stewardship of our resources, it is definitely time to "Go big or go home."

You are reading this book because you were born to "Go big."

INNER ACTION

We all want to see the "true riches" in our lives. We know we were born to do the impossible with God. But, we must steward what we have before we can increase in more.

The most potent weapon you have for change is vision. Vision is the fuel that we run on. It's the energy that creates action. Proverbs 29:18 declares, *"Where there is no prophetic vision the people cast off restraint."* Let God's vision for your future ignite a passion to steward your finances. Allow His dream for your life to awaken the desire to "get this money thing right."

1.   Find a quiet place to sit with a journal and a pen to record your answer to the following questions. As you write, be still and thoughts will come into your head that you did not originate.

- What is it you want to be known for in the Kingdom?
- What are some "impossible" things you want to see in your lifetime?
- What do you want to do?
- What is your dream?
- What is it you have a passion for?
- What do you feel called to?
- What is it you feel strongly about? Emotions are important. What you are angry about is a clue to what you are supposed to deliver. Moses got angry at an Egyptian overseer beating a Hebrew slave. Moses didn't know he was going to be a deliverer, but the anger was a clue. Your anger has to be channeled into a positive dimension.
- What do you love?
- What are you grieved over?
- What are you frustrated by? That is a clue to the freedom you are supposed to bring.

It has to cost you something. You are the one who has to pay the price to create the freedom. This revelation should drive you to fasting and prayer. This truth should inspire you to take care of that which is least—money.

2.   What price are you willing to pay to see God's dream for you come true?

Additional Resources

Dream Culture: Bringing Dreams to Life by Andy and Janine Mason
The Power of Your Life Message by Dave Crone

Endnotes

1. I first heard this principle taught from this passage by Andrew Wommack in a message called "Prosperity's First Steps" available at www.AWMI.net. He develops this idea further in Chapter 3 of his excellent book, *Financial Stewardship* (Tulsa, OK: Harrison House, 2012).

2. Ibid., 44.

3. Matthew 13:44-46.

4. John 14:12-14, Jesus says that we will do the works He was doing, and even "greater works."

5. I heard Bill Johnson make the statement, "The best way to distinguish between natural and true riches? Natural you can buy dinner and feed people, but with true riches you multiply one meal to feed thousands" in his message "Reformation Through Generosity." It inspired me to make the rest of the chart.

6. Matthew 9:25; 10:7-8; Luke 7:13-15; John 11:43-44.

7. Luke 22:49-51.

8. John 10:10.

9. Luke 4:18-21.

10. Matthew 6:10. There is no poverty in heaven.

11. Roger Sapp in *Radical Trust in God for Finances* (Southlake, TX: All Nations Publications, 2002) 52, 53, makes this great observation about this parable:

    While very few Christians doubt that Christ intends for us to increase spiritually, many Christians do not see the need to increase materially. Many are very passive concerning money and are not obeying the Master's words here with the assets He has given them. Christ has gone to receive His Kingdom and while He is gone, we should be doing business for Him with the financial assets that He has given us. Fear and greed do not motivate the true Christian steward but rather the desire to please the Lord and increase His Kingdom in the earth in every way. Stewards should seek a mighty increase through business in order to finance Kingdom works and to be generous in every way.

12. Dallas Willard, *Hearing God DVD* Session 2, "What Hearing God Is Not" (Downers Grove, IL: InterVarsity Press, 2012).

13. In light of the king taking from the servant who buried his money and gave it to the one who had the most, Bill Johnson commented that "Jesus is not a socialist." Message given August 13, 2014 at Voice of the Apostles.

14. Facebook post October 25, 2012.

15. Much of what follows in this section I learned from Bill Johnson's message "Brokers of Heaven" available at https://shop.ibethel.org. Used with permission.

16. Matthew 20:25-27.

17. This is a reference to the teaching on "The Seven Mountains" or "The Seven Mind-Molders" as a strategy to disciple nations. The teaching started with Bill Bright, Loren Cunningham, and Francis Shaeffer back in the 1970's. No one that I know of has carried that vision farther today than Lance Wallnau (www. LanceLearning.com).

18. http://kvministries.com/content/basic-training-prophetic-ministry-0. Accessed September 16, 2014.

Heaven Invading: Debt Cancelled

After a major surgery, we found ourselves owing over $20,000 in medical bills above and beyond what our medical insurance covered. I made a number of calls to the insurance company, as well as to the hospital, to discuss this large outstanding balance. We were hoping to negotiate a reduced amount, or better yet, persuade them to cover my bill entirely. Unfortunately, after numerous calls that were escalated to supervisors of supervisors, I was simply told, "Mr. Jewell, $2x,xxx is the amount you are responsible for." In other words, they left me with no hope of any possibility the bill could be reduced in any way, shape, or form. In addition to this news, they also informed me that the maximum length for a repayment plan is 24 months. After doing some quick math in my head, I determined there was just no way I could afford that kind of payment schedule.

It seems sort of comical now, but I recall complaining to God about this terrible financial situation. I explained to Him how I didn't have much (if any) savings and very little extra income to make payments with. I also filled God in on how faithful I was in paying my tithes and giving offerings, as though He needed reminding. I was very frustrated and stressed with the situation because I couldn't figure out how I could pay this debt.

The next Sunday at church, our pastor was raising money to tile the floor in the entryway. I remember thinking how I would love to help, but this huge medical bill that I already couldn't afford to pay was hanging over my head. The pastor asked those willing to donate to the project to raise their hand. Immediately, I heard the Lord tell me to pay for two sections. I tried to argue and then ignore Him, but I couldn't; I knew this was Him speaking to me. With a sick feeling in my gut, I held up my hand and indicated that I would pay for two sections. I was filled with peace.

Monday morning, the very next day, I received a call from the insurance company informing me that they reviewed our claim. They decided that although my request was beyond the scope of what my policy covered, they would pay the entire bill. I believe this great news was the result of my faithfulness to respond to the leading of Holy Spirit to pay for a couple hundred bucks worth of tile.

Eddie Jewell

CHAPTER 3

Who Can Take Better Care of Me Than Dad?

There are some days that are unforgettable. These moments create momentum; heaven marks you, your perspective is forever changed, and you are never the same again. This was one of those days.

When I was about eight years old, I remember getting into the "top drawer" of my father's dresser. Inside the dresser was his small wicker basket—a treasure trove of odds and ends. It contained exotic looking coins from all over the world, a small sewing kit, cufflinks, tie clips, different size batteries, golf tees, paper clips, mints—it was a tempting and beautiful bounty to my young eyes and fidgeting fingers.

One day, greed got the best of my little heart. The "looking without touching" became too much temptation for me to bear. I stole some of his "treasures" and put them in my top dresser drawer. Finally! They were all mine to have and to hold, to love and to cherish whenever I wanted.

A few nights later, dad tucked me in bed, and he started looking for something. He opened my top drawer and saw his "prized possessions" in there. "Jim, what is this?" he asked softly.

I knew I was busted. I could see the hurt in his eyes. I confessed that I had stolen his stuff.

Then the unexpected happened.

My father didn't give me a punishment or even a lecture. He gave me a revelation and an invitation. "Son, don't you know that everything I have is yours? Come here." Dad guided me to his bedroom and opened up his top drawer and explained, "You can have anything you want from here anytime you want."

I saw dad differently that day.[1] This experience shaped how I view my

Heavenly Father. God's love became my new plumb line.

My performance that day did not warrant a blessing. My father's great love for me was the basis of the blessing. I am a son—and that gives me access to everything! It always has and it always will. God is not dealing with you based on your performance; He is dealing with you based on Jesus' performance. That is the Good News of grace: Jesus got what you deserved so you can get what He deserves!

Jesus said, "Don't be afraid of missing out. You're My dearest friends! The Father wants to give you the very Kingdom itself" (Luke 12:32 MSG). Precious sons and daughters, do you know that the "top drawer" of the Kingdom is yours? Are you ready to start living like it?

BELIEVE AND RECEIVE OR DOUBT AND DO WITHOUT

Some people don't recognize this, but your impression of who God is determines how you receive from Him.[2]

> *May grace and peace be multiplied to you in <u>the knowledge of God</u> and of Jesus our Lord* (2 Peter 1:2).

Many people try to get grace and peace multiplied into their life through prayer or hands laid on them. The way that grace and peace is multiplied to you is *through the knowledge of God.*

> *His divine power <u>has granted</u> to us all things that pertain to life and godliness, <u>through the knowledge of Him</u> who called us to His own glory and excellence* (2 Peter 1:3).

This verse says that God's divine power has (past tense) given to us all things. Many are praying and asking God to send down His power from the outside, hoping for a spiritual bolt of lightning to hit them and then—BAM!—they are healed, delivered, prospered, or whatever they need.

However, this verse says that the "all things" pertaining to life and godliness come through the knowledge of God. This includes healing, prosperity, deliverance, joy, peace, favor, and anything else.[3]

Wrong knowledge will produce wrong results. If you aren't getting the results you desire, I can guarantee the root of that is some misconception or misunderstanding of God or how He deals with us. Instead of looking for prosperity to come externally, the first thing you need to do is recognize that the change begins on the inside of you. This occurs according to the knowledge that you have about God.

"Your impression of God will determine what you experience from God."

Regardless of what God is truly like, you are unlikely to experience God any greater than your concept of Him. I know that is a strong statement. God is who He is regardless of what you think. But your experience of God will be based on who you think God is and how He deals with us.

God will not be anything to you that you don't first believe Him to be. The Bible calls this faith, which is simply seeing things from God's perspective. Your impression *of* God will determine what you experience *from* God.

So, what is God like?

THE PLUMB LINE

Let's say you were going to build a wall. When you build, you have a plumb line, which is the standard by which everything else is measured. Of course, you want a plumb line that is straight.

During a mission trip to El Salvador, I noticed that on many of the buildings in the area, the builders didn't use a plumb line. I am not trying to make fun of them, but one wall went one way, while the other wall went another way; it was a mished-mashed mess. This is why plumb lines are critical—they ensure everything is straight, stable, and not an abstract funhouse. Everything is gauged by this truth. If the plumb line is off, then everything that follows it will be off. [4]

Jesus is the revelation of a kind of love the world had never dreamed. He is the plumb line for what God is really like (John 14:9). It took another Greek word to describe God's kind of love—*agape*. *Agape* is not an emotion that God has. It's His very nature—it is the way He is. *Agape* is the eternal choice of God to be for others, to exist for the good of His creation. [5] God doesn't just have love, God IS love—it's who He is and the way He is.

When I talk about God's kind of love, I'm not saying that His Love is greater than human love. His Love is nothing like human love. There's no comparison. *Agape* is not limitless human love or human love taken to some "super" level. There's an unbridgeable chasm between the best human love and God's *agape*.

You and I have love, so it can be more today than it was yesterday. It is capable of heating up and cooling down; it can fluctuate. But when we come to God, He *is* love. If God stopped loving He would cease to exist. His love will never change. He cannot be more love. He cannot be less love. God never wakes up in a bad mood.

God is **unconditional** love—that means He loves all people at all times

---

"God doesn't love you because of who you are; He loves you because of who He is."

---

under all conditions. God is love because that is the way that He is. God doesn't love you because of who you are; He loves you because of who He is. He loves you because "God is love."

GOD'S KIND OF LOVE VS. HUMAN KIND OF LOVE

Human love depends on the beauty and loveliness of the object of that love. When a teenager comes home from school and tells their parents they have fallen in love, what do they mean? Are they saying that they were walking around with an endless supply of love and they have now found someone to pour their tsunami of love upon regardless of that person's behavior, actions, or response? No.

When I fell in love with my wife, it wasn't because of the greatness of me and who I was, it was because of the greatness of her—she laughed at my jokes, was amazingly beautiful, and she liked martial arts and super hero movies. I had found the perfect woman! Human love depends on the beauty of the beloved. It is the beauty of the beloved that reaches out to you and awakens in you that thing we call love.

Because of this, so often we transfer that human concept of love to God and think God loves like we love. We think that when God sees you reading your Bible or praying or fasting, His heart beats faster and He "falls" in love with us. Until one morning you get up and you don't pray or you don't read your Bible and you think that God is through with you. God loves you with an infinite passion not because of who you are, but because of who He is.

> *Can a mother forget her nursing child? Can she feel no love for the child she has borne? But even if that were possible, I would not forget you! See, I have written your name on the palms of My hands* (Isaiah 49:15-16 NLT).

This is our plumb line; this is our true, magnetic north that we navigate life by. We order our life around the absolute of who God is. When a bill comes that you do not know how you are going to pay, you say, "I am facing this situation as if my Father really loves me and gave Himself for me. I am living in the absolute freedom that God is my Provider." There is no part of my life I can look at apart from the plumb line.

HOW FAITH WORKS

Galatians 5:6 says that faith works through love. There have been many times when I have tried hard to believe God for something when what I really needed was a greater revelation of God's love for me. Whenever you remove or decrease love, faith begins to waver.

I remember when Mary and I felt the Lord leading us from the marketplace back into vocational ministry. I had an encounter with the Lord one night where He made it clear that I was to leave the business I co-owned and become a senior pastor of a church. My last paycheck was April 2008. I knew we didn't have the finances to sustain us for the several months it would take to find the right church, move, and receive another paycheck.

A few weeks later I was "doing some business" with the Lord in prayer (Translation: I was complaining, crying and focused on my circumstance rather than God). I was stressed out and upset that I didn't see a way to provide for my family over the next few months. In between my sobs, a revelation of God's love came flooding over me. Any doubts about God providing for us melted away. I didn't know how. I just knew that He would.

As I paid bills and looked at my balance online, I noticed that checks were clearing, but the balance of our checking account stayed at about $6000. The balance was not decreasing. I called the bank and they said the amount was accurate. I told Mary, "I am not sure what is happening, but I think we are in the middle of a miracle."

For all of May, June, and July, I continued to pay bills and our checking account never went below $6000. When I started at Zion Christian Fellowship (the church where we now lead) at the end of July 2008 and received a paycheck, the checking account started decreasing, but only from the expenses from August on forward. For three months, God supernaturally sustained our checking account balance. It was like the widow's jar of oil that didn't run out (1 Kings 17:16).

I believe a deep revelation of God's love for us is the most important thing we can receive. Too many Christians let their feelings blind them to God's love. They are fighting with all they have to believe God is going to supply their needs, but their circumstances and feelings are screaming unbelief at them.

This is why we need frequent encounters and revelation of God's love for us. When His love floods over us, all the doubt about our needs being met melt away. When we know God loves us and is for our good in every situation, it becomes easy to trust Him. You may think you know God loves you; but if you are stressed out, worried, or have no joy—you do not believe God loves you.

Jesus revealed to us what God is really like. The Old Testament pictures of God are not inaccurate; they are just incomplete. Jesus is the complete revelation of what God the Father is like (John 14:9).

You have a heavenly Father who is absolutely crazy about you. You are the delight of His life, and He loves you as if you were Jesus Himself (John 17:26). In every situation that comes into your life, you now get to live in the light of that truth. You are constantly aware of His goodness; you are never doing anything by yourself or in your own strength and resources. You now can do things empowered by and in the strength of Christ.

To believe anything less is a lie and deception. It's not what Dad is really like. The person who has a "bad eye"—their heart and affections are anchored on "treasures on earth"—will not see or live in the reality of the Kingdom of God (Matthew 6:22-23). Some believers are moved more by their feelings than the character of God. Doing that is like a builder who ignores the plumb line and just builds a wall by their feelings, "I feel like it should go this way." And then the next day, they "feel" like it should angle the other way. Building by feelings will lead to an unstable mess.

I had a great opportunity to practice this truth in my own life. The week I preached a message regarding this subject, I got a call from my tenant. "The foundation of the house is crumbling," he said. Now, I am not expert on construction or structural engineering…but that didn't sound good! His bad news continued, "It's going to cost between $30,000 – $50,000 to fix it. Until it is fixed, the house is un-financeable, so it can never be sold." I was looking for a silver lining, but there was nothing about this conversation I liked.

"God is the absolute sneakiest Person in all of the universe, and I cannot wait to see what He is going to do."

Now, there is more than one way I could react to news like that. I could have freaked out, "Oh Mylanta, $50,000?! I don't have that right now! How are we going to fix this?"

But this time, I got it right. I said to Mary, my wife, "God is the absolute sneakiest Person in all of the universe, and I cannot wait to see what He is going to do." We took that house, and we put it in the river of God, "This house belongs to You. You are our Ultimate Source. I am sitting back, and I can't wait to see what You are going to do with Your house."

I was so confident God was going to act on my behalf, I told the congregation the story during my sermon the following Sunday. I added this declaration, "God will solve this problem by the end of this sermon series." I think it was two to three weeks later that I got a different call from my tenant, "I brought a friend out who is a real estate investor. He figured out a creative way to fix this problem…for $500." The tenant paid for it. It cost me nothing and the solution is a good and permanent one. Yea God!

When a difficulty hits, the first question is not, "What am I going to do?" Rather it is, "What should I believe?" Or, "Who has God said He would be for me?" Our beliefs don't change because our circumstances change; our circumstances change because our beliefs change.

THE PERFORMANCE TRAP

There are many ways the enemy tries to block the revelation of God's love for us. One of the most subtle, and therefore the most dangerous, is to deceive us into thinking God's love for us is tied to our performance.

Have you ever seen one of those old wells where you have to "prime" the pump? You put water into the suction valve to "prime" it with water so the pump functions properly. Many of us were taught that we have to "prime" the love of God—we have to do something in order to get His love to flow towards us—pray, fast, witness, give.

Religion is one of the biggest teachers of the "conditional-love-of-God" lie—that God's love for you is based on your performance. Giving is often presented as something you do in order to make God bless you. But the truth of the Gospel is that God blesses us because Christ has made us righteous, not because of our performance. When you believe you are loved and cared for, it is easy to be generous; as a result, God will give you more money to be a bigger blessing (2 Corinthians 9:10). Your actions didn't produce the relationship; your relationship to Dad produces the actions.

Grace is God saying, "I will carry My end, then I will carry your end, and I will treat you as if you had carried your end yourself."

SEE GRACE WHEN YOU SEE HIS FACE

So, what is grace?

Grace is the experienced reality of God's ongoing love and acceptance of us—which is not dependent on our failures or successes. Grace is God's desire to bless us—not on the basis of our performance, but on the basis of what Jesus "performed" on our behalf. Grace is not about what we have to do for God, but what God has already done for us.[6] Grace is God adding His ability to our availability.

Four hundred and thirty years after Abraham, the Law of Moses arrived—not to replace grace, but to show us even more that we need grace. The *Law* says, "I will carry my end, and I will bless you if you carry your end. But if you fail, I will curse you." God's Law was put in place to show us our need for a savior because our performance would never measure up.

The Old Covenant—the Old arrangement God had for dealing with man—was made obsolete, and a "New" arrangement came in. *Grace* is God saying, "I will carry My end, and then I will come and carry your end, and I will treat you as if you had carried your end yourself." God is saying, "I will bless you not on the basis of your performance, but on the basis of Jesus' performance on your behalf." That is the Gospel! That is the New Covenant! That is grace![7]

In the Old Testament, if someone had sin in their life and they brought a lamb as a sin offering, that lamb was carefully examined by the priest to see if it was acceptable (because the lamb could not be accepted if it had any kind of blemish). The priest did not examine the person who brought the offering, he only examined the lamb. In the same way, God does not look at us; He only looks at the Lamb of God to see if that Lamb is acceptable. And, thank you Jesus, the Lamb is acceptable.[8]

Jesus came to show us what God was like. Grace is not a doctrine—grace is a Person. When you encounter God, you encounter grace.

INHERITANCE: YOU GET WHAT SOMEBODY ELSE PAID FOR

Imagine if your great, great grandfather left you an inheritance before you were ever born. So you hit the birth lottery and get to enjoy this incredible inheritance that you didn't work for. Now imagine discovering this unearned wealth belongs to you and fearfully concluding, "Wow. I had better act really good so I can one day deserve this birthright and receive it." That would make no sense—trying to earn what was already yours. That's a picture of what religion does: it takes a free gift and puts a price tag on it.

There was an inheritance paid for you before you were ever born by your Father in heaven. You have access to His provision. You woke up into the blessing of the New Covenant. So, you don't have to say, "Oh, man, I'd better get my ducks in a row in order for You to bless me." It is already yours. Our response is simply worship, "Wow, I am going to live in the light of this inheritance." The proper thing for you to do is to start acting as if the inheritance was real (faith), to learn how to steward it, to multiply it to be a blessing, and to wholeheartedly and vibrantly live in the light of that truth.

The absolute standard, the highest and the best is Jesus. He shed His blood for you and paid for everything you will need to "reign in this life" (Romans 5:17). His covenant says, "I would rather die than to break My promise to you. Come live in the intimacy of Daddy's lap as My child."

GOD IS...

We've all heard 1 Corinthians 13—"the love chapter"—read at a wedding. "Love is patient. Love is kind…" Since God *is* love, this description of love is also a description of God. You need to know who God is for you. You need to know what God is really like. Look at the description of God we get when we substitute "God" for "love" in 1 Corinthians 13:4-8:

- "God is patient"—He never gives up on you.
- "God is kind"—He cares more for you than for Himself; He is the kindest Person in the universe.
- "God is not jealous"—He is not jealous of you, He is jealous for you to experience His goodness.
- "God does not boast and is not arrogant"—God humbled Himself and came as a baby, a dust-covered carpenter and revealed a Father.
- "God is not rude"—He doesn't force Himself on you; rather, He lets you choose what level of relationship you want.
- "God does not insist on having His own way"—He isn't "Me-first"— He is the ultimate servant.
- "God is not irritable"—He is faithful and never changes. You always know where you are with God because He never changes.
- "God keeps no record of wrongs"—The final clause of the New Covenant is "I will remember your sins no more" (Hebrews 8:12)!
- "God rejoices whenever truth wins out"—God is excited for you to come alive to all that you were created for.
- "God never gives up, never loses faith, He is always hopeful"—When we give up, God steps up and steps in with glistening hope and an expectation for good.
- "God endures every circumstance"—When you are at your worst, He is still at His kindest, most gracious, and completely for you.
- "God never ends"—His love for you doesn't decrease or increase, it is always on full blast!

You always know where you stand with God because His heart never changes towards you. He is the same on your best day as He is on your worst day. He doesn't believe in performance. There is nothing you can do to make God love you more, and there is nothing you can do to make God love you less. He doesn't love you because of who you are. He loves you because of who He is. This is what God is like.[9]

INNER ACTION

1.   It's time for a "Mind Bath." Read through the following verses slowly. Circle or underline key words that jump out to you. Write what God is speaking to you in your journal. God wants to give you new thoughts about who He wants to be for you and what He is like. Let these passages wash over your thinking and feed your heart and mind.

> *For if, because of one man's trespass, death reigned through that one man, much more will those who receive the abundance of grace and the free gift of righteousness reign in life through the one man Jesus Christ* (Romans 5:17).

> *Everywhere the sole of your foot will tread, I have given to you* (Joshua 1:3).

> *And my God shall supply every need of yours according to His riches in glory by Christ Jesus* (Philippians 4:19).

> *He who did not spare His own Son, but delivered Him up for us all, how shall He not with Him also freely give us all things* (Romans 8:32)?

> *For all the promises of God in Him are Yes, and in Him Amen, to the glory of God through us* (2 Corinthians 1:20).

> *And God is able to make all grace abound toward you, that you, always having all sufficiency in all things, may have an abundance for every good work* (2 Corinthians 9:8).

> *If you then, being evil, know how to give good gifts to your children, how much more will your Father who is in heaven give good things to those who ask Him* (Matthew 7:11)!

...those who seek the Lord shall not lack any good thing (Psalm 34:10).

Let them shout for joy and be glad, who favor My righteous cause; and let them say continually, "Let the Lord be magnified, who has pleasure in the prosperity of His servant" (Psalm 35:27).

The Lord will open to you His good treasure, the heavens, to give the rain to your land in its season, and to bless all the work of your hand. You shall lend to many nations, but you shall not borrow. And the Lord will make you the head and not the tail; you shall be above only, and not be beneath... (Deuteronomy 28:12–13).

The Lord is like a father to His children, tender and compassionate to those who fear Him. For He understands how weak we are; He knows we are only dust (Psalm 103:13-14 NLT).

As a young man marries a maiden, so will your sons marry you; as a bridegroom rejoices over his bride, so will your God rejoice over you (Isaiah 62:5 NIV).

Can a mother forget the baby at her breast and have no compassion on the child she has borne? Though she may forget, I will not forget you (Isaiah 49:15 NIV)!

The Lord your God is with you, He is mighty to save. He will take great delight in you, He will quiet you with His love, He will rejoice over you with singing (Zephaniah 3:17 NIV).

Moreover, because of what Christ has done, we have become gifts to God that He delights in, for as part of God's sovereign plan we were chosen from the beginning to be His, and all things happen just as He decided long ago (Ephesians 1:11 TLB).

And I am convinced that nothing can ever separate us from His love. Death can't, and life can't. The angels can't, and the demons can't.

Our fears for today, our worries about tomorrow, and even the powers of hell can't keep God's love away. Whether we are high above the sky or in the deepest ocean, nothing in all creation will ever be able to separate us from the love of God that is revealed in Christ Jesus our Lord (Romans 8:38-39 NLT).

My response is to get down on my knees before the Father, this magnificent Father who parcels out all heaven and earth. I ask Him to strengthen you by His Spirit—not a brute strength but a glorious inner strength—that Christ will live in you as you open the door and invite Him in. And I ask Him that with both feet planted firmly on love, you'll be able to take in with all Christians the extravagant dimensions of Christ's love. Reach out and experience the breadth! Test its length! Plumb the depths! Rise to the heights! Live full lives, full in the fullness of God (Ephesians 3:14-19 MSG).

Beloved, I pray that you may prosper in all things and be in health, just as your soul prospers (3 John 1:2 KJV).

How much do you think God wants your soul to prosper? That is how much He said He wants you to prosper in all things. Many will complain this verse is not speaking about money. I agree. It is talking about something much bigger than money.

2.   Some people have wonderful fathers like I did; others had no father in the picture or even an abusive father. Wherever you are on the scale, it doesn't matter. You are now set up to have an encounter with the Father to know who you are (identity) and why you are (the purpose for your life).

When you understand who the Father is for you, everything comes into place. Don't let your past experience of an imperfect earthly father keep you from the future experience of a perfect Father.

Pray this prayer throughout this week (adapted from Ephesians 3:18-19):

- "Holy Spirit come in revelatory power, show me how wide, how long, how high, and how deep the Father's love is for me."
- "Give me a series of encounters with the love of Christ so that I see

life from the Father's embrace."

Additional Resources

Experiencing the Father's Embrace by Jack Frost
From Slavery to Sonship by Jack Frost
The Supernatural Ways of Royalty by Kris Vallotton

Endnotes

1. I know some people may react negatively to that story because they want there to be punishment for sins; they think that it might teach kids that God excuses sin. Love changed me. It is the grace of God that teaches us to say no to ungodliness (Titus 2:11-12). It is the love of Christ that constrains us (2 Corinthians 5:14). God's love is the most powerful transforming force on the planet.

2. I first saw the connection between receiving from God and our knowledge of God from Andrew Wommack's teachings.

3. Andrew Wommack, *Effortless Change* from http://www.awmi.net/effortless_change/chapter_1 accessed on September 25, 2014.

4. I got the illustration of a plumb line as perfect love as related to Mammon from a sermon by Malcolm Smith, "In God We Trust" available at www.UnconditionalLoveFellowship.com.

5. Malcolm Smith, *Spiritual Burnout* (Tulsa: Pillar Books, 1995), 27.

6. Rob Rufus, *Living in the Grace of God* (London, Authentic Media, 2007), xi.

7. Ibid., 9.

8. Ibid., 17-18.

9. Graham Cooke, *The Church Has Left the Building* Disc 3. Available at www.BrilliantP

Heaven Invading: Checks in the Mail

My life changed immediately when I was born again and encountered the Holy Spirit; however, my finances did not. I was a few weeks from filing bankruptcy when I realized the Lord might have a financial system for me to discover. I studied the Bible and found dozens of verses that described how the Lord desires to bless us financially and show us that He is our source. I began to tithe, the first of several steps, and saw miracle after miracle occur in my life.

Each time I chose to be faithful to God it felt like the first time. There were times when I had to choose between the electric bill and the tithe. God showed me over and over again that He is my Provider.

A little while later, I gave a financial gift to a friend that needed it. When I got home there was a letter from my mother in the mailbox. My relationship with my mother was tenuous at best and strained even more since becoming a Christian. She was the last person I expected to receive money from.

When I saw the envelope I remembered a prophecy someone gave me that said if I continued to bless others with my finances, in one year I would have as much money in my checking account to equal the amount I owed in debt. This was around Christmas time, and I was working overtime and believing God to be completely out of debt. I had seen God provide a car, firewood, food, and rent, but I still had about $10,000 in credit card debt from college three years earlier.

When I opened the envelope I fell on my knees. There was no note of explanation, but there was a check for $9,900! I sat there in my hallway for about twenty minutes looking at that check in total shock. I prayed and thanked the Lord for meeting my needs again and asked the Lord to bless my mother. What made this method of provision even more astounding was that one month later, in January of the next year, she sent me another check for $9,900 to fulfill the prophesy of having as much money in my checking account as I had been in debt. God is amazing and is truly faithful!

Kurt and Sabrina

CHAPTER 4

Stepping into the Financial River

When I was about ten years old, our family went on vacation in New York to a place that had a small waterfall. There was a spot where you could jump off about a ten-foot cliff into the river below. The river water was brisk and its current was strong. You could hear the rushing sound even from a distance. After jumping in you had about twenty yards before the river deepened dramatically and increased in speed. There was a tall, skinny tree that lay across the top of the river that stretched from riverbank to riverbank; it marked where the river dipped several feet and the water speed increased significantly.

Our family stood on the edge of the cliff watching people jump in. They would plunge in and instantly come under the influence of the water's current. When they emerged, they immediately began swimming to the riverbank before the current carried them into the dip. Trust me—you do not want to get carried past that fallen tree.

It wasn't long before someone was unable to get to the riverbank in time. A college-aged girl who attempted this feat was not a strong enough swimmer, and it became clear that she was not going to make it to the safety of the riverbank after taking the plunge. She was swept downstream and was now hanging onto the wooden pole with her body dangling into the dangerous side of the river.

Then something happened that I will never forget: my dad jumped in to save her.

Our family watched from above as if viewing a slow-motion replay of a heroic moment. Risking his own safety, dad swam towards the screaming young woman. When he finally reached her, he somehow managed to pull her over to safety, snatching her from the clutches of the deep water's current.

She collapsed to the shore grateful to be safely back on land.

I learned a few lessons that day: 1) My dad is awesome. 2) Whatever gets put in the river comes under the influence of that river.

We see in Scripture Jesus talking about two masters: God and Mammon. Each master is like a river. Whichever master you choose to serve will put you under their influence. You cannot serve two masters at the same time anymore than you can stand in two rivers at the same time.

Where could the Kingdom current take you if you let yourself get swept away in the Father's love and care for you? And where have you seen Mammon's polluted currents drag people to?

THE POWER BEHIND MONEY——MAMMON

No one can serve two masters; for either he will hate the one and love the other, or else he will be loyal to the one and despise the other. You cannot serve God and Mammon[1] (Matthew 6:24 NKJV).

According to Jesus, it is impossible for us to give our hearts to two masters at the same time. That is like trying to walk in two directions at the same time. We must choose whom we are going to serve: *God or Mammon.* So what is *Mammon?* The word "Mammon" is an ancient Aramaic word that eventually held the idea of trusting in money.[2] Mammon is not money, but a demonic principality working to abuse money. The Bible doesn't say you can't have money. It says don't serve that principality.[3]

You cannot serve God and Mammon (Matthew 6:24 NKJV).

The word "serve" describes a servant or slave; someone whose actions are being directed by someone else.[4] One Greek scholar described "serve" in this way:

This word was used to denote *a servant who had become a slave for the rest of his life.* This servant's lifetime responsibility was to "service" his master with all his attention, time, and energy. In other words, he catered to his master's every wish, desire, and demand. He was there to help, assist, and fulfill his master's wants and dreams to the exclusion of all else. This servant's entire existence was to "service" his master in whatever way the master asked or demanded.[5]

One of my hobbies is detailing cars. I love the "detail" in "detailing." That means I give attention to every part of the car: I clean the wheel wells, dress the tires, polish the exhaust tips, treat the leather, protect the carpet, clean in between the air conditioning vents, and vacuum under the seats. I wash my car once a week, but every year I give it "the works." This treatment includes claying, polishing, and sealing the paint. It requires time, attention, energy, and money in order to "service" my cars.

When Jesus told us, "You cannot serve God and Mammon," He was telling us that both God and Mammon require time, attention, energy, and money. Mammon wants to be your master in the same way God does. Which one we serve shows up in the "detailing" of daily life. Jesus knew there is not enough of you and me to properly "service" both God and Mammon in our lives. Once our decision is made, we must then "hate the one and love the other."[6]

"Your dollars are like soldiers that you are in charge of to command to do Kingdom business."

A love for God is sometimes measured by what we hate. You love one and you hate the other. Or, you will be loyal to one and despise the other. If you are loyal to Mammon, then you will despise every time the subject of money is brought up in church. You forget that the resources of the world are here for Kingdom purposes. If you are loyal to God, you will enjoy every time finances are taught on just as much as identity, healing, the finished work of the Cross, or the goodness of God. You remember that your dollars are like soldiers that you are in charge of to command to do Kingdom business.

BOWING OUR KNEE TO A LESSER GOD

"But Jim, I would never 'serve' Mammon. I am a Christian. My heart is fully for God."

There is a way that we as believers—you, me, pastors, missionaries—can worship this god. Everyone reading this book has done it. When we worship

Mammon, we look to money for security, meaning, and identity. We give money our affection, loyalty, and service. Someone who worships Mammon looks to money the same way a believer should look to God. I changed the wording in some popular Bible verses to illustrate this point. Are you ready?

- "Where does my help come from? My help comes from money."
- "Money is my shepherd. When I have it, I shall not want."
- "Even when I walk through the valley of the Shadow of Death, money will comfort me."
- "Money is an ever-present help in time of need."
- "Money gives me peace that passes understanding."
- "People perish for a lack of money."
- "My money shall supply all of my needs."
- "A day in the mall is better than thousands elsewhere."

If you feel better about yourself and more confident when you have money, then you are not getting your identity from God, you are getting it from Mammon. If you feel a little more secure at night because your bank account is getting fatter, you are under the influence of Mammon.

Here is the lie behind Mammon: *"Get real. God doesn't really care for you; God doesn't really love you. He is concerned about all those big shot, superstar Christians, and we all know that's not you. You are just a nobody. Your puny life isn't going to change the world. Those biblical promises may work for other people, but I've never seen them work for you and you haven't either. If only you had money, then you wouldn't have to worry. You could make a name for yourself. If you had a better place to live, people would like you, you'd have friends, and you'd have the influence you deserve. If you had money, people would finally respect you—even your family. Money is all you need to finally be safe, secure, and happy. Enough of this scraping by, get what you can and hold onto it. And we'll be laughing all the way to the bank. Now that's a life!"*

The goal of Mammon is to make you think "I MUST have money and lots of it. The "daily bread" thing won't cut it. I have got to have bread for my tomorrow and my tomorrow's tomorrow. And when I have money, I am going to spend lots of time and energy trying to figure out how to never lose it." These thoughts begin to consume you, giving you proof that the current of Mammon's river is getting stronger. [7]

Remember, "God IS love" (1 John 4:8). The life of God is love, so when you give money to God, you are giving it out of love. If I give an offering because I feel guilty or obligated, that is not love. If I give in an offering because I think I can get even more money back, that is not love. If I do something nice for my wife just so she will do something nice in return, that is not love. That is called selfishness, manipulation, and bribery.

The spirit of Mammon twists our giving to God, "*If* I do give anything away, I need to have a guaranteed return on my investment. I will give to God only on the condition that you will show me how He will give it back, because I can't afford to let money fly out of my pocket like that.

There are Christians in the church who have partnered with the spirit of Mammon, believing that they were sowing a seed, when in reality they were making an offering to Mammon. "If I give away all I have, and if I deliver up my body to be burned, but have not love, I gain nothing" (1 Corinthians 13:3).

Love says: "I can't help but give. No use in trying to stop me. I am going to give, and I am going to love it." You can give without loving, but you cannot love without giving. "I am going to give because You are my Source. I am investing my life and my money in Your Kingdom. It's all yours anyway, and that's how I want it. You are my Dad, and I wouldn't have it any other way."

WORRY IS TO MAMMON WHAT WORSHIP IS TO GOD

> *Therefore I tell you, **do not be anxious** about your life, what you will eat or what you will drink, nor about your body, what you will put on. Is not life more than food, and the body more than clothing* (Matthew 6:25)?

Jesus is simply saying that if you understood the treasures available to you in the Kingdom of Heaven, you would never again be anxious. But when your attention, focus, and heart become caught up in a lesser kingdom, the only result will be anxiety, worry, and frustration. Worry is temporary insanity because it is imagining a future without God. The words "anxious" and "worry" both have reference to strangling or being choked, which is the feeling we get when we are anxious. [8]

What praise and worship is to God, anxiety and worry is to Mammon. Both are a pledge of allegiance. When we lay down at Jesus' feet in worship, we are saying: "There is no God like You; You are awesome. When I look at

"Worry is temporary insanity because it is imagining a future without God."

You, I am at peace. You are where I get life, strength, fulfillment, security, and joy."

When you worry over clothes, when you worry over your job, when you worry over the mortgage payment, retirement, the kids' college tuition—when you are anxious and fretting, you are giving praise and worship to your master, Mammon. You are saying, "There is no god like you; you are awesome. When I look at you, I am at peace. You are where I get life, strength, fulfillment, security, and joy." Only, you are giving it to the wrong master.

Mammon's purpose is to capture your heart by convincing you that money is what you should be pursuing. It tries to put a deep fear in your heart that you are not going to be taken care of, that you are not going to have enough money, so you must spend a lot of time and energy pursuing and acquiring it.

When Christians hear about a conference on "Supernatural Finances" they often think, *"I hope this person tells me how to get more money because I don't have enough. More money will solve all of my problems. The real power is in money."*

The truth is that the power is found in God. That's a huge part of what makes Him God. The power is not in money. You don't need more money. You need more relationship with the Source.

Mammon hits you two ways: fear and greed. It can deceive people of great wealth and little wealth. Fear says, *"There isn't going to be enough."* Greed says, *"I don't have enough. I NEED more!"* They are both using the same lie, *"God is not enough. You need to grab the bull by the horns and you need to take care of this yourself because He isn't going to."* It is the same lie; it just manifests itself in the different ways. Both are worship to Mammon.

Worship is not what you do on a Sunday morning, *"I go to church to worship so I can get filled up."* Worship is recognizing who God is, *"You are awesome. You are good,"* and as a result of that I get *"filled up."* In worship, I declare it with my mouth, and then I declare it with my life by lining up with the truth that Perfect Love has set Himself *for* me in every situation. That is how I worship Him, that is how I step into the financial river. I put every situation under the influence of God, who IS love. Any other thinking has to have repentance.

Repentance is recognizing I need God's plumb line because my wall is all over the place. Repentance isn't, *"I am sorry for this, I am sorry for that, I am sorry that this board is crooked, God."* Repentance is saying, *"I need to tear down the whole wall and start over again because there is a whole new way to live; God is for me and I get to live in light of that."*

Here is one of the best verses of the Bible in regards to how loving God really is. Here is how you now get to think about everything; this is your lens for seeing circumstances:

> *He who did not spare His own Son but gave Him up for us all, how will He not also with Him graciously give us all things* (Romans 8:32)?

If God did not spare His own Son for us, then surely He will take care of all our needs as well! So when you are faced with daily questions like, "What am I going to wear? What am I going to eat? How will I make my mortgage payment? Will I get this job? Will I keep my job? Will I get this commission? Will I get that promotion?" Then you no longer think about things apart from the One who delights in giving "good gifts" (James 1:17). You are jumping into and becoming under the influence of the Kingdom River.

"Every time you worry, you are bowing your knee to a lesser god."

Worry only comes from believing the wrong things; it comes from an inadequate knowledge of God. Worry is like cancer of the mind. Every time you worry, you are bowing your knee to a lesser god.

You can now live under the influence of the "Kingdom River" in any situation you may face in life. This is the relationship Dad is offering to you. How should you respond? It is the *"Thank you!"* of faith. That is worship—I see who God is and I declare it with my mouth and then I declare and display it with my life. I face any situation in the light of this Father, who is perfect love, who rejoices over me with singing, [9] who is the fruit of the Spirit—love, joy, peace, patience, kindness, goodness, faithfulness, gentleness, and self-control. [10] Anything less is a lie, a deception.

INNER ACTION

1. Do you remember the *"You might be a redneck if…"* jokes, made popular by the comedian, Jeff Foxworthy? *"You might be a redneck if…for you, possum is the other white meat."* In the spirit of that, here are some, *"You might be under Mammon's influence if…"* Circle any that apply to you.

- You think about all of the things you could buy if you didn't give.
- You don't give in the offering because you think you can't afford it or are afraid you won't have enough to meet your needs.
- You get jealous or can't celebrate someone else's financial testimony.
- You watch TV shows where people win money and dream about you being that person.
- You constantly complain about the economy or the price of gas.
- You look for a career based on how much money you will make rather than what God's calling is on your life.
- Money is causing problems in your marriage.
- A good deal of your thought life is spent thinking about things you don't have but that you want, or things you already have that you want more of, or in a better or newer version.
- You frequently have this thought, "I don't know where the money went."
- Even though you make more money than you used to, you still don't seem to have enough.
- You buy things you don't need because they were a "good deal."
- You're afraid that every preacher is out to get your money.
- You have balances on your credit cards that you can't pay off each month.
- You constantly compare your clothes, tech, car, and home to your friends or celebrities and go into debt to stay "on trend" with them.

2. Pause and ask the Holy Spirit to reveal where the spirit of Mammon has influence over your mind, heart, and emotions. Look back over some of the numbers you circled above and talk to Him about those areas.

3. Renounce any agreement you have formed with the spirit of Mammon. Declare in your own words, *"I renounce any agreements I have made with Mammon. I break that power over me in Jesus' name!"*

4.   Repentance means changing your mind to see things from God's perspective. It means to think differently. Ask God to forgive you for worry and anxiety (it is a sin). Write down some of the truths of this chapter (maybe you already underlined them) that stuck out to you. Meditate on these things as you go throughout your week.

5.   What physical reminder can you set before you this week that you are "Stepping into God's financial river"? (For example: change the background of your computer or phone to a picture of a river.)

Additional Resource

Wealth, Riches & Money by Craig Hill and Earl Pitts

Endnotes

1. Some modern Bible translations have the word "money" instead of "Mammon." Usually those translations have a note that acknowledges that the original New Testament Greek word is "Mammon."

2. D.E. Garland, "Mammon" in *The International Standard Bible Encyclopedia* Vol. 3 (Grand Rapids, MI: William B. Eerdmans Publishing Company, 1986), 232.

3. I don't believe that Jesus' reference to "Mammon" means "money." If "Mammon" means money then you should renounce it and have nothing to do with it. Poverty would be the answer, and that clearly is not what the Bible teaches.

    There is some debate as to whether or not "Mammon" was a false god during Jesus' day. Regardless, Jesus paints a picture of Mammon as a potential idol, a false god; an alternative to the one true God. Ephesians 6:12 states, "For we do not wrestle against flesh and blood, but against the rulers, against the authorities, against the cosmic powers over this present darkness, against the spiritual forces of evil in the heavenly places [or spiritual realm]."

    Hill and Pitts (14) believe Mammon fits the category of a "cosmic power" or "spiritual force" in the spiritual realm that influences the hearts of people to love and serve money in the physical realm. I agree.

4. "*Douleúō*" in *The Complete Word Study Dictionary: New Testament*, ed. By Spiros Zodhiates (Chattanooga, TN: AMG Publishers, 1992), 482-483.

5. Rick Renner, *Sparkling Gems from the Greek* (Tulsa, OK: Teach All Nations, 2003), 436.

6. Ibid.

7. Trusting God does not negate wise planning; it just means you don't put your trust and security in wise planning.

8. Willard, 209.

9. Zephaniah 3:17.

10. Galatians 5:22-23.

Heaven Invading: Debts Paid Off

We had more than $80,000 in debt (not including our mortgage) when we learned the Lord wanted to be part of every facet of our lives—including our finances. We made a conscious decision to put God first in every part of our lives and came up with a plan to be out of debt in three-and-a-half years.

As soon as we made this plan and committed ourselves to putting God at the center of our finances, everything changed. Our marriage improved, I got a new job, money started pouring in, and we began tithing with an open and excited heart.

Earthly calculations showed we would be out-of-debt in three-and-a-half years but God had other plans. Supernaturally, we were out-of-debt in eight months! Cars, credit cards, and home equity line of credit all gone. Thank You Jesus!

Mark and Cara

CHAPTER 5

WARNING: Don't Confuse Your "Source" with the "Resource"

eing a prophet was a rough job in the Old Testament. God sometimes had them perform little object lessons for the Israelites to make His messages clear. God told Isaiah to walk around naked for three years.[1] He told Hosea to marry a prostitute.[2] Ezekiel was commanded to cook his food over human dung.[3] Maybe that is why the church has been a "non-prophet" organization for so long!

Do you remember Elijah, the prophet?[4] God had him prophesy that there wasn't going to be any rain for years in the land...the very land he was living in![5] I'd be thinking, *"God, wouldn't it be better to prophesy this drought over someone else's land, where I am not living? Maybe one of Israel's enemies?"* God provided a new resource for Elijah, *"Don't worry, Elijah, I've got this. What you need to do is go to the brook Cherith. You can drink the water from the brook, and I have a special delivery service set up to bring you breakfast and dinner every day."* Elijah was in close enough relationship with God to hear that and know His voice.

> *"Our Source of provision never changes, but our resource for provision can change frequently."*

Everything was going great and then...the brook dries up. What happens to most Christians when their brook dries up? They start freaking out. *"God*

51

has abandoned me! What are we going to do?" Every time there was a change in the resource of provision for Elijah, here was the very next phrase, *"Then the word of the Lord came to [Elijah]."* [6] When your resource of provision stops, what should you be doing? Maybe you could make this statement, *"I need the word of the Lord. I need to know where my new resource of provision is coming from."*

Here is what Christians need to understand: our Source of provision never changes, but our resource for provision can change frequently. When you know that no one can take better care of you than Dad, if you were to walk into work tomorrow and your boss were to hand you a pink slip, your blood pressure doesn't even need to go up. Your thought can be, *"God, you are the sneakiest Person in the universe. I can't wait to see how You are going to work this thing out."* No one can take better care of you than Dad.

So the brook dries up on Elijah, and here we see the sneakiness of God in action, "Elijah, go to the city of Zarephath and look for a *widow*." [7] Elijah had to be thinking, "Did You say look for a *window*? Like a *window* of blessing? God, is this a metaphor?" God is like, "No, *widow*."

"God, is 'Widow' the name of a rich man, like a Joseph-type of guy who had stored the grain for the famine?"

"No, she's a widow."

In those days, widows were not a good resource for provision. Women couldn't really work. A widow is someone whose resource of provision had already dried up—her husband.

So Elijah goes to Zarephath and finds a widow looking for some twigs and leftover stubble to start a small fire. That's not a good sign. [8] The conversation then goes something like this:

Elijah asks the widow, "Could you bring me a drink of water?" As she goes to get him the water, "And while you are at it, can you get me something to eat too?"

She replies, "Not really. You've caught me at a bad time. I don't have any food. All I have left is a little bit of flour and oil. My plan was to gather a few twigs to make a little fire for my son and me so we can bake one last little cake...that we may eat it and die." Obviously, this is not the declaration of faith the prophet wanted to hear from his new resource of provision.

As I read this, I am expecting Elijah to say something like this, "Here's the plan: I am going to find some people with money in this town and take up an offering for you. After all, you only have one meal left, and then you are going to die." And I would be way off base.

The prophet does something interesting here instead. He does take up an offering…for himself! "Go ahead and make the little cake as you planned, but bring it to me first." Can you just see the newspaper headlines the next day, "Prophet of God Takes Last Meal from Widow"?

Why did Elijah have her bring him her last cake? Was it his scheme to get a free meal? The real question is, "Where was the widow putting her trust?" The answer is: in the flour and oil. The spirit of Mammon had already gripped her heart. She was thinking, "When that flour and oil run out, I am dead." Mammon shouts that your life is dependent upon the resources that you have available in your hand, your bank account, job, parents, and your 401K.

The point Elijah is making to this widow is communicating to her and us that our life is not dependent on flour and oil. Our life is dependent on the living God. He is the Source of provision, but our trust has to be in Him, not in "flour and oil." So how did he break the trust in flour and oil? By having her give away part of the last bit of her resource. Neither God nor Elijah was after her flour and oil. God was after her heart and faith. God wanted to be her Source of provision.

I believe a similar dynamic is seen when preachers receive offerings today. Some people feel churches are after their money. Some may have the wrong motives, but I believe that most of the time a preacher is not after people's money. He and God are after their faith. Faith in God releases miracles.[9]

When the widow did what Elijah asked her to do, it released a supernatural miracle of provision from God. Once her hands let go of the flour and oil they became free to take hold of Daddy's hand and Daddy's plan! The oil and flour did not run out "for many days" (1 Kings 17:15). She learned to live by trusting the word of the Lord instead of material possessions. God became her Source.

BUT WHAT IF I RUN OUT?

I remember when God was teaching me this lesson. We had some upcoming expenses and were excited to be able to pay cash for it. As I sat in a church service, God prompted me to give away everything in our savings account to an impactful ministry, including what we had saved up for the upcoming expenses. The prompting came to me with that kind of "scary excitement." It felt like an adventure with God. I talked it over with my wife and we agreed it was God inviting us to do this. (It is *very* important to be on the same page with your spouse in financial decisions—that golden nugget may have been worth the price of the book!)

And it was settled.

We emptied out our savings account and wrote the check. I nervously gave it away. Within two weeks, I received all of the money back from an unexpected resource. Yea God! (Disclaimer: I don't believe God always rewards obedience that quickly. If He did, Christians would see Him as a divine ATM machine and miss out on developing Christ-like character while waiting for the blessing. Other times, I have had to wait longer and I am waiting on the Lord right now. Our attitude needs to be that of wonder regardless of the timeline, *"I can't wait to see what God is going to do here!"*)

Out of that testimony, God showed me something pretty amazing that I am still trying to live out. Our church has seen a number of people physically healed. When I lay hands on someone to see them healed, I am never afraid of running out of healing anointing. The thought never crosses my mind, *"If this person gets healed, I may not have enough anointing to see the next person healed."* Why does that thought never cross my mind? Because when I pray for healing, I am keenly aware that the Source for healing does not come from me. I am tapping into a Source of limitless supply.

And yet, when I have a check in my hand, sometimes there is a hesitation in my heart, *"If I give this much, we may not have enough for…"* God began to challenge me to see giving the way I see healing. When I am prompted to give, I do not need to fear that I will run out. It's His healing power in the first place. And it's His provision to begin with. God is Jehovah Jireh—the God of Limitless Supply.

I was talking to Craig Hill (probably my favorite author on finances) one day, complaining about how Mammon kept "sneak attacking" me. I thought I had dealt with it, but it kept popping up. Craig said that it is like trying to keep a soccer ball submerged in a swimming pool—the ball is always trying to rise to the surface and get on top of you. He said the soccer ball is money, the air in the ball is the spirit of Mammon. When there is a lot of air in the ball, you have to continually shift your weight and attention to stay on top of it and not let it get on top of you. When there is no air in the ball, it is easy to stay on top of it. Whatever you don't manage, manages you.[10]

Unfortunately, this is a lesson we must learn again and again as believers. Most of God's tests are pop quizzes.

WHY "SOWING SEED" HASN'T WORKED LIKE WE THOUGHT

For years, I have thought about, prayed about, and wrestled with the Bible's teaching on "sowing a financial seed" (2 Corinthians 9:6-15). When I read the following scenario in *Wealth, Riches & Money*, it connected so many dots for me.[11] If you have ever been in a Spirit-filled type of church, then you have probably heard an offering received something like this:

"Who here needs more finances in their life?" (Crowd raises their hand or shouts "Amen!")

"Well, according to Scripture, poverty and lack are *not* God's will."

"There is a biblical principle of sowing and reaping" (cue the scriptures from Mark 4 or other passages on the projector screen).

"If you have a need, then you must sow a seed (money) into the offering. God wants to return that back to you 30-, 60-, or 100-fold."

Have you ever wondered why this doesn't seem to be working? How many Christians do you know who are regularly seeing a multiplied return on their giving?

It *is* true that poverty and lack are not God's will. He is the Father who "delights in giving good gifts to His children" (Matthew 7:11). One of His names is "God our Provider"—Jehovah Jireh. The biblical principle of sowing and reaping *does* apply to money. God does want to multiply back financial seed. So what is the problem? To hopefully save you years of toil and frustration, I'll tell you.

The problem with this approach to giving is **it reverses our relationship with God.** I become the master and God becomes my servant that I use to get me more money. Craig Hill describes this:

> *"You don't have enough money. We are going to use God and God's principles to get you money. When you have money, then you will be OK." NO! God is not the servant to get you money. Money is your servant to expand the Kingdom. God is your Master. You are His steward called to manage money under His direction...We are to use money to serve God, not use God to get money.*[12]

The first time I read Craig Hill's above statement I about fell out of my chair! I know there have been times I have bought a Christian book on finances where my goal was to learn how I could get God to give me more money. I hoped it was just me. Sadly though, many Christians have become angry with God or with Bible teachers by attempting to operate in the principles of sowing and reaping, when they haven't first established the "Foundation for Supernatural Finances" discussed in this book.

DON'T "SOW A SEED TO MEET YOUR NEED"

In Matthew 6, Jesus explains why we never need to be anxious and then gives a model for how provision is going to come to us. You and I have heard it taught for years that the way provision will come to you is by giving. The principle is sowing and reaping. "If you have a need, sow a seed." The idea is that when I give, it is going to release provision back to me. Here's what's interesting: this *isn't* Jesus' model. He actually teaches *against* that.

What's the model Jesus uses for provision? Birds.

> *Look at the birds of the air: they neither sow nor reap nor gather into barns, and yet your heavenly Father feeds them. Are you not of more value than they* (Matthew 6:26)?

What did Jesus just say? "…they neither sow nor reap"—that is the exact opposite of what I was always taught to do. He is saying, "Don't do that. That is not how provision comes to you." What else does Jesus tell us not to do? "…nor gather into barns." They don't hoard, save, or store. They don't sow and reap. Then how in the world are they provided for?

"No one can take better care of you than Dad."

You can almost hear Jesus saying this with a little smile, "How many birds are you worth? Five cockatoos, a hawk, two doves, and a bald eagle?" Here is the point: provision comes to you from God for one reason and one reason only—**because your Father in heaven loves you more than birds.**[13] No one can take better care of you than Dad. If you are wondering if God is going to provide, step outside. If you see birds who aren't starving to death,

God still loves you and will provide.

When our kids were little and we were driving down the road, we used to tell them every time we saw a bird, "There is a reminder that God is going to take care of everything we need." Use this in your own life. Every time you see a bird, let God's love and care for you wash over your heart and refresh you.

Craig Hill calls this "Sparrow Faith"[14]—a basic trust that God will provide for my needs because He loves me. If we don't have this as our initial foundation, any other biblical principles of finance are easily distorted by Mammon and used to confuse people.

"Sowing and reaping is a correct biblical principle. It is just not supposed to be used to get your needs met."

I am *not* saying that financial sowing and reaping with an expectation of return is wrong. Sowing and reaping is a correct biblical principle (I'll devote a chapter to this in *How Heaven Invades Your Finances Book 2: Revolutionize Your Living, Giving & Receiving.* It is just not supposed to be used to get your needs met. The way this principle is frequently taught makes the meeting of your needs dependent on your works and not upon God's love and grace.

Have you noticed that you have never heard a news report about the thousands of birds that are found dead all over the world from starvation? Have you ever seen an anorexic bird? No. Have you see the birds freaking out or having an anxiety attack lately over provision? No. But the Christians sure are. Why are these birds at such peace? What do they know that we need to learn? They have an inner revelation that *"my Father in heaven loves me. Ahhhhhh. I can rest. I am going to be okay. And that means I can soar."*

Jesus uses another picture: little children (Luke 11:11-12). How much time does your little four-year old child or grandchild spend thinking about provision? Do they lie awake at night thinking, *"Am I going to have food or clothes tomorrow?"* No.

Why? Because they know, *"I have a mom, a dad. They love me."* That's all they know. They don't even know where food comes from. Something called "the store." How do you get it out of a store? I don't know. Mom and dad just bring it. Food appears. Clothing appears. This house appears. All of this stuff appears for one reason and one reason only: daddy and mommy love me and that is all I need to know.

Can you imagine how offensive it would be to a parent if that little child got the idea that her provision depended on her sowing and reaping? Can you imagine that little four-year old coming to her parents with fear and tears in her eyes, *"If I give a tithe of my peanut butter sandwich at lunch, can I please have dinner?"* The parents would say, *"Honey, do you really think that your dinner is dependent upon you giving away one-tenth of your lunch or not? Giving away part of your lunch to someone who doesn't have one is a noble thing. But I want you to know that you will always have dinner whether you give your sandwich away or not. Because of one reason and one reason only: I love you!"* [15]

WHO'S YOUR DADDY?

I believe the whole difficulty of seeing the supernatural in our finances (or any other area of our life) has everything to do with our understanding of the Father. We don't believe that He is as good as a good earthly father (the Bible calls this "unbelief") when in fact, He is infinitely better.

Jesus said:

So if you sinful people know how to give good gifts to your children, how much more will your heavenly Father give good gifts to those who ask Him (Matthew 7:11 NLT).

Jesus is inviting us to compare what a normal parent would want for their children with what the Father wants for us. If we would not do something harmful or bad to our own children, then the Father will not do it to us either. If we would not injure or make our children ill, then the Father will not injure or make us ill either. If we would not leave our kids hungry and without provision, then He will not leave us hungry either. This principle cuts through complex theological thought that confuses good with evil. If common sense says that the circumstance is bad, then our Father is not doing it to us. [16]

The Father will abundantly provide, save, heal, and deliver us through Christ reliably and consistently. This is certainly not mysterious for anyone who really knows our Father. It is because we are greatly loved.

God is not just *able* to help, He is actually *eager* to help. The church is His bride. We are His sons and daughters. You will sleep a lot better at night once you nail down this truth in your life. God is the ultimate supplier for the resources we need and He desires to bless His children. And He has plenty. [17]

"God is not just able to help, He is actually eager to help."

Picture a baby sleeping happily in his parent's arms. That child doesn't have any worries. He is just resting in the lap of love of his parent. Jesus is inviting you into a dimension of living where you can rest in your Abba, Daddy's lap of love; a life free from worry over money.

As you go to work, it is with the absolute freedom in your heart that says, *"This job was given to me by my Dad."* And if your employer stands at the door with a pink slip, you take the slip and you go on your way, trusting the One who says, "I will give you your 'daily bread'" (Matthew 6:11). Your employer is not your Source; they are just a resource. If that job changes, your attitude is, *"God is the sneakiest Person in the universe, I can't wait to see what He is going to do."*

After all, who can take better care of you than Dad?

INNER ACTION

I want to take an offering. Before your blood pressure goes up, let me explain. I want you to give your worries to God.

1. Get a piece of paper or a note card and write down the issues, situations, bills, etc. that are weighing down on you.

    Give all your worries and cares to God, for He cares about you (1 Peter 5:7 NLT).

    - Now take that list and give it to God. Go through each item with the Lord and declare that He is "Lord over _____" (fill in the blank with that item). When you are finished, throw the list in the trash as an act of faith: "I give all my worries and cares to God, for He cares about me!"

2. To "meditate" means to think brilliantly about God. It is to allow His thoughts to permeate your mind, will, and emotions so that your reflex is to think like Him.
    - Find a place of stillness before God. To prepare yourself to hear from Him, you may even pray the prayer of Samuel, "Speak Lord, for your servant is listening" (1 Samuel 3:9). Take your time. When you find that place of rest in the Lord, enjoy it. Worship Him there. Be with Him there.
    - Read Philippians 4:4-9 and Proverbs 3:5-6 two times each (on next page). Look for the word or phrase that strikes you. Write this down in your journal or a sheet of paper.

3. Read through the passages two more times. This time, listen for the way in which the word or phrase you just wrote down connects with your life right now.
    - Ask yourself, *"What aspect of my life does this word or phrase speak to?"*
    - After reading, pause for at least one minute to listen. In the silence that follows, listen to God for the connection between this word and your life.

4.   Read through the passages a final two times. During this reading, listen for God's call to action. "Is there anything God is asking me to do in response to what I have just heard?"

- Pause for at least three minutes of silence afterwards. Listen to God's invitation to you and talk to Him about what you are hearing. As honestly as you can, let Him know what you are thinking and feeling. Express any concerns or questions you might have to Him.

Celebrate God all day, every day. I mean, revel in Him! Make it as clear as you can to all you meet that you're on their side, working with them and not against them. Help them see that the Master is about to arrive. He could show up any minute!

Don't fret or worry. Instead of worrying, pray. Let petitions and praises shape your worries into prayers, letting God know your concerns. Before you know it, a sense of God's wholeness, everything coming together for good, will come and settle you down. It's wonderful what happens when Christ displaces worry at the center of your life.

Summing it all up, friends, I'd say you'll do best by filling your minds and meditating on things true, noble, reputable, authentic, compelling, gracious—the best, not the worst; the beautiful, not the ugly; things to praise, not things to curse. Put into practice what you learned from me, what you heard and saw and realized. Do that, and God, who makes everything work together, will work you into His most excellent harmonies (Philippians 4:4-9 MSG).

Trust God from the bottom of your heart; don't try to figure out everything on your own. Listen for God's voice in everything you do, everywhere you go; He's the one who will keep you on track (Proverbs 3:5-6 MSG).

Additional Resources

Lessons From Elijah by Andrew Wommack

Endnotes

1. Isaiah 20:2-4.

2. Hosea 1:2.

3. Ezekiel 4:9-13.

4. I heard Craig Hill preach a message about the spirit of Mammon at Zion Christian Fellowship on February 2, 2013 where he used the Elijah story to illustrate how God can make provision for you without using money.

5. 1 Kings 17:1.

6. 1 Kings 17:2, 8.

7. 1 Kings 17:8.

8. On 1 Kings 17:10, "The woman is gathering twigs to start a small fire. The verb suggests foraging for discarded stubble. The traffic through the town gate and jostling of loads there would make it a likely place for one to find small pieces that had been dropped by others" in *The IVP Bible Background Commentary: Old Testament* by John Walton, Victor H. Matthews and Mark W. Chavalas (Downers Grove, IL: InterVarsity Press, 2000), 376.

9. Craig Hill, *Living on the Third River* (Littleton, CO: Family Foundations International, 2002), 39.

10. Personal phone conversation, July 2014.

11. Craig Hill and Earl Pitts, *Wealth, Riches & Money* (Littleton, CO: Family Foundations International, 2001), 19-20.

12. Ibid., 20.

13. Craig Hill sermon, Zion Christian Fellowship, February 2, 2013.

14. Craig Hill, *Living on the Third River*, 28.

15. Craig Hill sermon at Zion.

16. Adapted from personal notes from a sermon given by Roger Sapp at Zion Christian Fellowship, November 2008.

17. Bill Hybels reminded me of this in *Courageous Leadership* (Grand Rapids: Zondervan, 2002), 99-100. Chapter Five, "The Resource Challenge," is a must-read for pastors.

Heaven Invading: Commissions

While my wife was pregnant with our first child, she lost her job. She was a public school music teacher and her school was shut down. At the same time, I was transitioning from receiving a salary to commission. We had all of those natural concerns about needing income, starting a family, and provision. I was in a tough business, where out of the ninety-five people hired in my recruiting class, 90% had failed out.

I was raised in a home where we grew up understanding and praying for the favor of God in our lives. Three months into the job, I cold called a business client and won a $40 Million account. This was unheard of for someone so new and so young. They were my first client and have since grown into over a $100 Million account.

I doubled my income that year, replacing the income we lost. Seeing God's faithfulness gave me the confidence to survive as a rookie. This testimony of God's favor and provision marked our family at a time when we had virtually no money.

Couple in their 20's

CHAPTER 6

An Invitation to Financial Freedom

S tuff. We see Stuff on TV. We see other people's Stuff. We want Stuff. We buy Stuff. We have "Black Friday" and "Super Sale Saturday" for Stuff. We polish it. We charge it. We rent storage units for it. We insure it. We compare our Stuff to other peoples' Stuff. Stuff has a way of getting a hold of us.

It's sobering to observe how early our possessions start possessing us. When children reach about two-years old, they only have a few "go to" words and phrases. The timeless toddler favorite? "No!" Want to guess what the other word is? "Mine!" It always amazes me when a two-year old says, "Mine," because they didn't earn any of this Stuff. It was all a gift. They can't even take care of it very well. Their Stuff could be taken away in an instant. The Stuff is not really theirs at all. It's just an illusion, but a pretty strong one. Two-year olds can be funny that way, but grown-ups can be too.

As we get older, we keep collecting, buying, thrifting, and amassing more Stuff than we have room or need for. We know a family who has an annual tradition of doing a garage sale each summer. They accumulated enough Stuff that they could literally fill their front yard with Stuff to sell *every* year. It became so regular that they bought clothes racks, display tables and even had a giant board with a color-coded dot system for pricing. It was set up better than some chain stores. It was like an outdoor Wal-Mart (without the self-checkout kiosk).

Studies show that about one-half of all Americans have credit card debt that they do not pay off each month.[1] Even so, we still want more Stuff. Nations go to war over it. Families are torn apart because of it. Friendships sometimes end because of it. Success and identity are measured by it. People spend their lives worrying about it. Husbands and wives argue more about

Stuff than any other issue. Prisons are full of people who committed crimes to acquire more Stuff. [2]

In high school, for some strange reason, I prided myself on the fact that I never read a book all of the way through the four years. During my junior year, we had to give an oral book report for English class, which I completely forgot about. Imagine my surprise when my friends reminded me about it during lunch—only thirty minutes before it was due. So, I did the only thing that came to mind—I made up a book. I invented the title, author, and story during lunch (luckily this was before the internet, so getting caught in this was more difficult).

I gave the report and then faced something unforeseen—questions about the book from the class—which included the inquisition from my goofy friends who knew what I had done. "So, what was the most unexpected part about the book?" "Tell us more about how the characters were developed," they prodded. I fought them off with replies like, "The book was so good that I don't want to spoil it for you." Somehow I made it through that day with my dark secret intact and the teacher none the wiser. (Disclaimer #1: Do not try the above story at home! Disclaimer #2: I am a bit more "saved" now then I was then.)

Despite my academic success without reading, something strange and unexpected happened to me when I was in seminary: I developed a love for books. I became a reading machine. I would skip meals during the week and use the money to buy books every Friday at the used Christian bookstore in town. I spent hours going through the Christian book catalog that was sent to my house, circling commentary sets I wanted and prioritizing my purchases. I started getting prideful over my book collection, which was now in the hundreds.

There was another student at the seminary who was bitten by the "book bug" as well—Anthony. He would race me to the used bookstore and taunt me with his bargains. I started going several times per week on the days they stocked the shelves with new books. I can't count the number of times Anthony and I locked eyes going down the book aisles in search of our next prize. We were like rival treasure hunters competing for lost gold. Then Anthony threw down the gauntlet: he got a job at a local Christian bookstore where he could get 40% off books. I knew I couldn't compete with that. I was crushed. I cursed that day.

I was the first of the two of us to graduate from seminary and work at a church. The church I served gave me a generous book allowance. As our libraries grew, Anthony and I would mail each other pictures of our books (it was the 1990's) to see who had the bigger collection (not to rub it in, but my library is now bigger!). I would sit in my office and look at the walls now lined with over three thousand books and feel like they were my personal "cloud of witnesses" cheering me on. I felt a real connection to Gollum in *Lord of the Rings* when he found, "My precious!"

Then tragedy began to strike—people in the church found out about all of my books and wanted to *borrow* them. "No!" Was my immediate mental reflex, quickly followed by "Mine!" Not only were people borrowing them, but worse than that, they were not returning them.

I hatched a plan to remedy this injustice. I had my secretary send out notices to people to return the books by a certain date. One person returned the books he borrowed with a cartoon attached. It was a picture of two old men chained to a wall next to each other. He crossed out the caption and added his own dialogue, "What are you in for?" The other man replied, "I didn't return Baker's books." [3]

I guess it's not just two-year olds who struggle with "Mine!"

"I EARNED IT; IT'S MINE!"

Whose Stuff is it anyway? Is it my Stuff, or is it God's Stuff? Who is the Owner? You may be thinking, *"I am the one who worked fifty to sixty hours for the money I have. I toiled most of life working two jobs. I worked hard for it. Mine!"* It may seem like reality, but it's not true.

"There is no such thing as a self-made person."

A story is told about the CEO of a large Fortune 500 company who is driving along with his wife. They pull into a service station. Since it's a full service station, an attendant comes over to fill up the tank. The husband goes in to pay the bill and comes back to find his wife engaged in a rather animated conversation with the service station attendant. The husband gets in the car, and as they drive away, he asks her, "What were you two talking about?"

She tells him that she knows this guy pretty well. As a matter of fact, he's her ex-boyfriend. The CEO is feeling somewhat smug about this blast from the past. After a while he says to her, "I'll bet I know what you're thinking. You're thinking that you're glad that you married me, the Fortune 500 CEO, and not a service station attendant."

And she says, "No. Actually I was thinking that if I had married him, he would have been a Fortune 500 CEO, and you would have been a service station attendant."[4]

There is no such thing as a self-made person.

God gave you life. He is the Source of every good thing in your life (James 1:17). He gave you the mind and gifts and talents you use to earn a living. He set you in the most prosperous time in the history of the world. Even though you work hard at your job, God is still the Source of your financial success. Without God's blessing on your life, you wouldn't even have the ability to prosper.[5] It is just like the two-year old who thinks all the toys belong to him. In reality, they are just the blessing of a loving parent.

There is a story in the Old Testament when David was the king of Israel. He started off as a shepherd boy and probably didn't have much Stuff. Then he became king of Israel during a time of unbelievable prosperity, so as king, he had a lot of stuff—even his stuff had stuff.[6]

One day as David is sitting in his house made of marble and gold, he thinks about how God doesn't have an appropriate house to be worshiped in. God's presence dwelt in the "Ark of the Covenant"—which was a box with a few reminders of their history with God in it.[7] Then David gets this idea:

What if I were to use my Stuff to serve and honor God? What if I were to build a temple where people would walk in and say, "Wow!"? Not because they were impressed with the decadence and design, but because it would be a place where they could be reminded of the goodness, greatness, and the closeness of this God who gives manna and takes care of people's needs.[8]

So David tells God that he would like to build Him a house. God basically says, "David, you can't, because you have led too violent of a life as a warrior to build a house for me. But your son, Solomon can. Just not you."[9]

Now, I don't know about you, but if I were in David's place and I poured out my heart to God with an idea to worship Him and He said, "No," I'd be tempted to pout a little bit. I'd want to take my ball and go home. But David has a totally different response. Since David can't build the Temple, he leads the way in giving for the resources for the Temple, as told in 1 Chronicles 29.

Out of the national treasury that he controls as king, he provides the gold, silver, bronze, iron, wood, precious stones and marble slabs. He described his giving as with "all my might" or "all my abilities" (verse 2). But King David isn't content to just give from the national treasury, he gives out of his own wallet—over $4.5 billion in gold! He gives an additional $160 million in silver (verses 3-5).[10]

David then issues a challenge, "Who then will offer willingly, consecrating himself today to the Lord?" (verse 5). In other words, who else is willing to give like this? It's interesting that David didn't command them to give. Kings in those days didn't ask, they took. David, however, knew God was building a different kind of community. Stuff only means something if it's given with a joyful heart.[11]

There was an explosion of generosity where the people gave over $7.5 billion in gold in addition to silver, bronze, and iron. Look at the words used to describe the heart behind their giving:

Then the people <u>rejoiced</u> because they had given <u>willingly</u>, for with a <u>whole</u> <u>heart</u> they had offered <u>freely</u> to the Lord. David the king also <u>rejoiced</u> greatly (verse 9).

The people actually wanted to do this. This is a community who wanted to give. There is rejoicing. Why? Because they understood the difference between Stewardship and Ownership. Listen to David's prayer:

And David said: "Blessed are You, O Lord, the God of Israel our father, forever and ever. Yours, O Lord, is the greatness and the power and the glory and the victory and the majesty" (verses 10-11).

And then David says these words (if we could only get this in our hearts):

...for all that is in the heavens and in the earth is Yours (verse 11).

What is David saying?

God is the Owner. I am a steward. God has entrusted me with some Stuff. It's not my Stuff. Somebody had it before me; somebody else will get it after me. I'm going to go. For a little while, I manage it. It's God's stuff.[12]

In fact, David went on in his prayer:

Everything comes from You, and we have given You only what comes from Your hand (1 Chronicles 29:14 NIV).

This truth is all through the Bible:

The earth is the Lord's, and everything in it. The world and all its people belong to Him (Psalm 24:1 NLT).

"The silver is Mine, and the gold is Mine," declares the Lord of hosts (Haggai 2:8).

You shall remember the Lord your God, for it is He who gives you power to get wealth (Deuteronomy 8:18).

You are not your own, for you were bought with a price (1 Corinthians 6:19-20).

We are like two-year olds giving presents to their parents when we give money towards the Kingdom. It all belongs to Him; He even owns me. As author Randy Alcorn says, "God never revoked His ownership, never surrendered His claim to all treasures. He didn't die and leave the earth to me or anyone else." [13]

GOD IS THE OWNER, I AM HIS MONEY MANAGER

Understanding that "God is the Owner" is only half of the lesson; the other half is recognizing that "I am His money manager." You need to adopt a steward's mentality toward the assets He has *entrusted*—not *given*—to you. [14]

There are two great words in the Christian vocabulary—"steward" and "stewardship." Jesus had several parables about stewards. In each parable, the owner or master represents God or Christ and the steward represents each believer.

A steward in the New Testament times was a person who managed someone else's property, finances, or other affairs and were not owners of the property they managed. God entrusts His things and His wealth to those specially tested servants who are genuinely and acutely aware that they own nothing. [15]

I want you take a moment to picture the FedEx driver delivering packages. Can you see him in his purple shirt? The giant white truck with the word "FedEx" on the side? I am in awe of this guy. He gets it. He spends dozens of hours each week driving around town giving away packages to people like it is nothing. He doesn't seem worried about himself. His focus is on getting packages to other people.

I have never had him give me a package and tell me about what a great sacrifice it was or how he wrestled with FedEx over delivering it, and after all that decided to anyway. He doesn't even seem concerned with having a limited supply. It's like he knows when his truck is empty, there will be more packages supplied from FedEx. I know if that was me, I would be thinking, *"What if I run out of packages? What if there is not enough for tomorrow? I could be out of a job!"* But not this guy! He just keeps giving away and giving away these packages. What is he doing? He recognizes that he is not the owner; he is just the delivery guy. The packages don't belong to him.

What would you think if instead of delivering the package, he took it home and gave it to his wife? *"My wife loves this store; I think I'll keep this for myself."* If the delivery guy begins acting like the owner, there are problems; jail time kind of problems.

Until you recognize that "God is the owner, I am His money manager," nothing else the Bible says about finances will work for you.

When you think that the money comes by the sweat of your brow, then you keep a much tighter hold on it. If I am the owner, then giving is an obligation. Then I want someone to tell me what the rule is for giving. When someone asks, "Should I tithe on the gross or the net?" Here is what they are really asking, "What is the least amount I can give and not have God mad at me? How much of my Stuff can I keep and not get into trouble?" Mine!

Until you recognize that "God is the Owner, I am His money manager," *nothing else the Bible says about finances will work for you.* As long as you are holding on to your money with a clenched fist and have the priority of your finances on yourself, God's method of prosperity won't work for you. You have to change your mindset to recognize that God is the Source of everything you own, and you are the steward of those financial blessings He has given you.[16]

Another way of saying, "God is the Owner, I am His money manager" is "Jesus is Lord over my finances." Jesus is either Lord of all, or He is not Lord at all. If God is not first in your finances, He is not first in your life.

CHRIST'S RADICAL MESSAGE ON FINANCES

The biblical concept of stewardship is strange and radical to our modern American lifestyle. Unfortunately, "stewardship" is often associated with committees, programs, or fundraising. Some people label themselves a steward in an attempt to justify their stinginess instead of giving liberally. Jesus taught about the radical nature of stewardship in two short parables:

> *The kingdom of heaven is like treasure hidden in a field, which a man found and covered up. Then in his joy he goes and <u>sells</u> <u>all</u> that he has and buys that field.*

> *Again, the kingdom of heaven is like a merchant in search of fine pearls, who, on finding one pearl of great value, went and <u>sold</u> <u>all</u> that he had and bought it* (Matthew 13:44-46).

Jesus uses two pictures to describe the heart condition of a person who chooses life in the Kingdom with Jesus. The believer discovers something of infinite value and sells all he owns to obtain it. The treasure is of course Christ Himself. The person senses that this is the opportunity of a lifetime

---

"This is the heart of a disciple—seeing that following Jesus is the opportunity of a lifetime."

---

and he does not want to miss out. Do you think the businessman who found the pearl was sweating over its cost? Do you think the one who found the treasure in the field—perhaps oil or gold—was thinking about all that he had to give up to get this? The thought never crossed their minds.

Their thinking is more like, *"I get to receive the entire Coca-Cola company, but I have to give up this can of Diet Coke in my fridge…it is SO worth it!"* This passage is not about the cost; it is about having clarity about the bargain. The only thing these people were sweating about was whether they would "get the deal." This is the heart of a disciple—seeing that following Jesus is the opportunity of a lifetime and is worth giving up everything for that prize. [17]

DISCIPLESHIP 101

There is a stupid and sadistic teaching out there that asserts if you give your life completely over to God, it is going to be miserable. He'll have you serve in a malaria-filled swamp under a vow of silence and poverty. If you serve God fully, then anything you love in life is over. Unfortunately, much of this comes from the misunderstanding of Jesus' words about being His disciple:

> *If anyone comes to Me, and does not hate his own father and mother and wife and children and brothers and sisters, yes, and even his own life, he cannot be My disciple. Whoever does not carry his own cross and come after Me cannot be My disciple. So then, none of you can be My disciple who does not <u>give up all his own possessions</u>* (Luke 14:26-27, 33 NASB).

People took these verses and boiled them down to, "If you don't hate your life and give away all of your Stuff, you are not a disciple; therefore, God will make you hate your life and force you to live in poverty so you can be His suffering servant and true disciple." But, Jesus was not saying that misery and lack are the hallmarks of a disciple.

When my two oldest sons were in fourth and fifth grade, I coached their basketball team. Now, these kids were not interested in learning the basics of dribbling, passing, and shooting. They wanted to move onto the more advanced techniques that were much more impressive: like three-point shots, dribbling between their legs, and around-the-back passes. Much like me trying to teach my boys the basics of basketball, Jesus is saying to His players, "Verily, verily I say unto thee, if you can't learn to dribble down the court, you will not be able to do a hard crossover dribble, go behind your back and through your legs when someone is guarding you." You can imagine a teacher saying to her students, "If you can't learn the alphabet, you won't be able to learn to read Shakespeare."

Jesus is giving them Discipleship 101: "As long as you think anything may be more valuable than fellowship with Me in My Kingdom, you cannot learn from Me." If you don't see the value of following Christ enough that you would surrender your identity, your life, and even "all of your possessions," you will never get the basic points about life in the Kingdom. Giving 10% out of habit is not what Christ is after. We must renounce all ownership of all wealth and possessions. We must become obedient stewards.[18]

> So then, none of you can be My disciple who does not _give up all his own possessions_. Therefore, salt is good; but if even salt has become tasteless, with what will it be seasoned? It is useless either for the soil or for the manure pile, it is thrown out. He who has ears to hear, let him hear (Luke 14:33-35).

Sometimes stewardship does look like missions, sacrifice, or selling all of our Stuff. But, knowing the infinite value of following Jesus makes it all worth it. That's the heart He wants to cultivate in us—unconditional love and unconditional obedience. Without this kind of commitment, everything else for Christ is useless and shallow. We will be salt without taste. We will be useful for nothing.

THE "SECRET" TO 100-FOLD RETURN

Jesus encountered a man who is described as being rich, young, and a ruler.[19] He approached Jesus and wanted to become a follower:

> "Teacher, what good deed must I do to have eternal life?" And He said to him, "Why do you ask Me about what is good? There is only One who is good. If you would enter life, keep the commandments." He said to Him, "Which ones?" And Jesus said, "You shall not murder, You shall not commit adultery, You shall not steal, You shall not bear false witness, Honor your father and mother, and, You shall love your neighbor as yourself." The young man said to Him, "All these I have kept. What do I still lack?" (Matthew 19:16-20).

After answering some questions, Jesus got right to the heart of this man's issue for becoming His follower:

Jesus said to him, "If you wish to be complete, go and sell your possessions and give to the poor, and you will have treasure in heaven; and come, follow Me" (Matthew 19:21 NASB).

Jesus gives this man three-fold instructions:

1. Sell all your possessions.
2. Take the money you get from selling everything and give it to the poor.
3. Follow Christ.

Why didn't Jesus just tell him to give everything away? That would have been a lot quicker and less painful. Jesus gives him a process that would require him to die each time he sells something for the sake of his relationship with God. Every sale and gift to the poor would liberate him from the Mammon spirit. He would then be free to be able to become Christ's disciple and wholeheartedly follow Jesus without hindrance. The rich young ruler will become a true servant and a steward of Christ if he *sells all*. [20]

When the young man heard this he went away sorrowful, for he had great possessions (Matthew 19:22).

The rich, young ruler claimed to know the Law and the prophets. If he really did, he would have known promises like, *"Whoever is generous to the poor lends to the LORD, and He will repay him for his deed"* (Proverbs 19:17). If he really knew what the Old Covenant said, he would have known the Lord would repay him for everything he gave away.

The rich young ruler was unwilling to sell all to follow Jesus. He wanted an internship experience with a popular teacher, not a Lord who demands sacrifice. His plan was to continue to trust in wealth for security and meaning in life. Seeking financial security is self-centered and focuses on what a person can acquire. Jesus was offering this man something much more: the true financial freedom that comes from turning over your finances to God.

Jesus already had twelve "interns." How does their response to following Jesus differ from the rich, young ruler?

Then Peter said in reply, "See, we have left everything and followed You. What then will we have?" (Matthew 19:27).

I want you to stop and let that hit you. The disciples already passed the test. Remember, "leaving behind everything" to follow Jesus is basic

Discipleship 101—normal Christianity. It's the only response that makes sense when you see the pearl of great price and the treasure hidden in the field. The Owner has the right to tell you what to do with His Stuff. An idol in your life is anything you have to first ask permission from before obeying Jesus. Peter asks, "Jesus, we have already put our total trust for our families, our financial futures—everything in Your hands. What do we get?"

> *Jesus said to them, "Truly, I say to you, in the new world, when the Son of Man will sit on His glorious throne, you who have followed Me will also sit on twelve thrones, judging the twelve tribes of Israel"* (Matthew 19:28).

In other words, the disciples will not experience the full impact of the rewards of following Christ until the age to come. In that age, they will have an important position and function because they left everything behind to follow Him. [21] But then Jesus makes an additional promise that can apply to *all believers* who meet its conditions:

> *And <u>everyone</u> who has left houses or brothers or sisters or father or mother or children or lands, for My name's sake, will receive a hundredfold and will inherit eternal life"* (Matthew 19:29).

What had the disciples left? Houses, brothers, sisters, fathers, mothers, children, property. [22] They left behind the resources of family and property—all of their Stuff. They already passed the Discipleship 101 test of stewardship when they followed the command of the Owner to leave behind their livelihoods and resources. Now, Jesus promises that "everyone" who sacrifices everything now for Christ will receive an eternal reward as well.

Just in case you think this is just a promise of heaven, compare it to what Jesus says in Mark 10:

> *Jesus said, "Truly, I say to you, there is no one who has left house or brothers or sisters or mother or father or children or lands, <u>for My sake</u> <u>and for the gospel</u>, who will not receive a hundredfold <u>now in this time</u>, houses and brothers and sisters and mothers and children and lands, with persecutions, and in the age to come eternal life* (Mark 10:29-30).

Many people try to claim a "100-fold" return on their giving based on this verse. Giving does not fulfill the conditions of this promise; just being willing to give doesn't fulfill it either. Only leaving all for the right reasons ("for My sake and for the gospel") fulfills the conditions. Motivation is important. You cannot leave everything behind, or sell all so that you can gain wealth, position, or prestige. God does reward faithful and tested stewards with more to take care of, and they can expect to see ongoing supernatural increase and unusual supernatural intervention by Christ in their finances. However, we don't seek these things directly. We seek to love people and follow Christ.

"Giving all or leaving all for the wrong reasons will profit you nothing. You will not be a true steward unless you get rid of selfish motivation."

If I give away all I have, and if I deliver up my body to be burned, but have not love, I gain nothing (1 Corinthians 13:3).

Giving all or leaving all for the wrong reasons will profit you nothing. You will not be a true steward unless you get rid of selfish motivation. [23]

A FINANCIAL EUNUCH

You may be thinking, "What in the world is a financial eunuch?"[24] Well, let's start with a physical eunuch. A eunuch in the ancient east was a man who had been castrated; so as a result he had no sexual desire. His role was to serve with the king's harem. The harem was made up of the most beautiful women in the land, who were dedicated to the king.

Any guesses on what would happen if a man touched one of the women in the king's harem for himself for physical pleasure? He would be killed. These women were dedicated for the king alone. Because eunuchs had been totally stripped of the desire to take the bride for themselves, they were given the exclusive job of working with and preparing the bride for her king.

A financial eunuch is:

...someone whose primary role is to handle financial resources for the King. He/she would never touch this resource for self, as this desire has already been dealt a deathblow...So a financial eunuch is a person who comes to the Lord, applying for the job of managing and handling a fiduciary account on behalf of the Lord for the purpose of expanding the Kingdom of God. [25]

You can see why renouncing the spirit of Mammon (Chapter 4), recognizing God as our Source (Chapter 5), and seeing God as the Owner and yourself as the manager is so important. As long as you are holding onto your money with a clenched fist and acting like the owner, God's method of prosperity won't work in your life. You have to recognize that God is the Source of everything you own.

There will be a day when we stand before God and give an account for our lives, a sort of job performance evaluation (Romans 14:10, 12). Our name is on God's account. We have unrestricted access to it. If we think like owners, we are abusing that privilege. When we think like stewards or investment managers, we always look for the best place to invest the Owner's money; that life will be rewarded. [26]

My favorite worship leader, Mary Baker (my wife), wrote a song that summarizes the heart behind a steward. Here are some of the lyrics:

> I will give all, to pursue the depths of You.
> I lay down all, to gain what I can't lose.
> I give it all, I give it all, I give it all. [27]

THE INVITATION

I was talking to a friend of mine when he said, "Jim, I am a millionaire" (everyone loves that part of his testimony). "There have been three times in my life where the Lord has asked me to give away everything" (people aren't usually as excited about that part). He has given away cars and not had a ride home. He had kids in college counting on him to make the payments when the Lord had him give away all the money in their accounts.

He told me how his father was a shrewd businessman who was very conservative with money and thought his son was crazy for being so generous. At the end of his father's life, his dad was rebuking him for being so generous. My friend asked, "Dad, how much money do you have in the bank after all of these years of saving, conserving, and investing?" His dad told him the amount. "Dad, I have three times the amount that you have."

Here is the part of our conversation that hit me like a FedEx truck, "And Jim, I can't wait for God to ask me to give it all away again! I'll have more stories." That is the heart of a steward. He knows whose Stuff it is. That is a man who is completely free from Mammon and isn't worrying about money.

God is inviting you to experience the freedom of turning your finances over to Him. When Christians think that when it comes to money, it is all up to them, they often struggle financially. God never intended for you to carry the burden of finances. He wants to lift that burden off of you. Whatever hole you are in financially, it is not a grave! Even if you dug it yourself through poor choices, God will climb in there with you and walk you out. It may not happen with one check coming in the mail, but He desires for you to be debt free and outrageously generous.

INNER ACTION

1. As a steward, you must answer the question, "How much is enough?" Otherwise, any increase will typically be used for personal consumption. A family that has decided how much is "enough" can receive increase and pray about the purpose of the increase and not assume that it is for personal consumption (although it may be a blessing from the Lord for them to enjoy). The best plan that I have seen for this is Chapter 6 "Close the Circle" in Craig Hill's and Earl Pitts' book, *Wealth, Riches & Money*. I encourage you to buy it and walk through this crucial process. It is available at www. FamilyFoundations.com.

2. How we handle money indicates what we *really* believe, not what we *say* we believe. What do your actual day-to-day patterns regarding money indicate that you really believe with respect to the following statements? On each continuum, place an X where you see yourself.

☐ The priority of my finances is on me

☐ The priority of my finances is on God and others

☐ My money belongs to me

☐ My money belongs to God

☐ I get jealous when others get blessed

☐ I rejoice when others get blessed

☐ Money has little to do with my spiritual life

☐ Money is an indicator of my spiritual life

☐ When I get unexpected money I think about what I can buy

☐ When I get unexpected money I think about giving or investing

☐ I decide where my money goes

☐ I receive guidance from the Holy Spirit about where His money goes

☐ Living a blessed life is optional

☐ Living a blessed life is required

☐ Being broke keeps me dependent on God

☐ Recognizing my Source keeps me dependent on God

3.   How does your current handling of money demonstrate that God is important to you? Be specific.

4.   Earlier you read:

Another way of saying, "God is the Owner, I am His money manager" is "Jesus is Lord over my finances." Jesus is either Lord of all, or He is not Lord at all. If God is not first in your finances, He is not first in your life.

Take some time, with your spouse and family if applicable, and dedicate your finances to God. Maybe take your wallets and checkbooks and declare, "Jesus is Lord." Feel the peace that comes with turning your finances over to God.

5.   I bought our church business cards with "God is the Owner, I am His money manager" written on the front. I challenged them to put this card in front of their debit card in their wallet to remind them that God is the Owner before they made a purchase. What practical reminder can you put in your life to keep this freeing truth before you?

Additional Resources

Financial Stewardship by Andrew Wommack

The Treasure Principle by Randy Alcorn

Radical Trust in God for Finances by Roger Sapp

Endnotes

1.   The number was 46.7% as of December 30, 2012 according to http://www.nerdwallet.com/blog/credit-card-data/average-credit-card-debt-household accessed on August 28, 2014.

2.   This "Stuff" part of the introduction was adapted from a message by John Ortberg called "Stuff Part One: Who is the Owner?"

3.   For the record, God dealt with me about holding on to things too tightly and I started giving away books like crazy. Since then, I have given away hundreds of books. Almost every time I part with one, I still think about that cartoon and smile.

4.   Ortberg, "Stuff Part One: Who is the Owner?"

5.   Andrew Wommack, *Financial Stewardship* (Tulsa, OK: Harrison House, 2012), 16.

6.   I heard John Ortberg use the story of David building the temple in his message "Stuff Part One: Who is the Owner?" which inspired me to use it here.

7.   Hebrews 9:3-5 tells us that in the ark was the golden pot of manna, Aaron's rod that budded, and the tablets of the covenant (these were copies, as Moses smashed the originals). Each element in the Ark of the Covenant embodied a physical revelation God gave to His people. The "golden jar of manna" embodied the revelation of God's supernatural provision for them. The rod of Aaron represents the revelation of God's mark of delegated authority among the people. The story of Aaron's rod budding (Numbers 17:8) revealed that God's appointed leadership must always be identified by the manifestation of resurrection life. The tablets of covenant expressed His encounter with them on Mount Sinai and memorialized the covenant made between God and His people. See Bill Johnson, *Release the Power of Jesus* (Shippensburg, PA: Destiny Image, 2009), pp. 57-66 for more on this.

8.   John Ortberg in his message "Stuff Part One: Who is the Owner?"

9.   1 Chronicles 28:1-8.

10. One talent of gold is equal to about 75 pounds. So, 3000 talents x 75 pounds x 16 ounces x $1260/ounce of gold (price at the date of this writing, 9-8-14) = $4,536,000,000. 7000 talents of silver x 75 pounds x 16 ounces x $19.20/ounce price at the date of this writing) = $161,280,000.

11. Ortberg.

12. Ortberg.

13. Randy Alcorn, *The Treasure Principle* (Colorado Springs: Multnomah Books, 2001), 24).

14. Ibid., 25.

15. Roger Sapp, *Radical Trust in God for Finances* (Southlake, TX: All Nations Publications), 2002, 5-6. Roger Sapp notes that there are some who may react to this truth of servanthood or stewardship because we are also called sons and daughters. He continues that this is partly true and partly false. Our sonship does not negate the truth that we are still called His servants or in some places "bondslaves." We must hold these truths in balance.

16. Wommack, 24.

17. I first saw these passages as getting "clarity about the bargain" from Dallas Willard, *The Divine Conspiracy* (San Francisco: HarperSanFrancisco, 1998), 292-294.

18. Roger Sapp (p. 20) warns that before you feel motivated to give everything away, you need to be reminded that all wealth and property belong to Christ. The Owner alone has the right to tell us to give it to someone else. In other words, a steward that gives everything away better be absolutely sure that he is doing it in obedience to the command of the Owner and for no other reason. God always rewards obedience. He does not reward stupidity or fanaticism. Christians who foolishly give away everything without Christ's command are bad stewards and will have less to take care of and no promotion from God. When I teach on giving in *How Heaven Invades Your Finances Book 2: Revolutionize Your Living, Giving & Receiving*, I will give some guidelines to insure that it is Christ that is commanding and not a foolish impulse or a suggestion from the devil. So for now, patience, reflection, prayer, and study are recommended over action.

19. The account of the rich, young ruler is told in Matthew, Mark, and Luke. No one account has all three characteristics (rich, young, ruler), but all three characteristics appear in the three gospels.

20. Sapp, 25.

21. Sapp, 30.

22. Roger Sapp has an important footnote here (Note 5 p. 31), "We note that no wives were left behind. Because of this, it stands to reason that no small children were left behind either. Christ's statement here must mean only grown children. There are several Greek words that mean exclusively small children. They are not used here. However, the Greek word "*tecknon*" that is used here doesn't reveal age at all, only relationship."

23. Sapp, 34. He goes on to give some advice on "Protection from Abusers" (35). Roger warns that some may try and abuse the message of stewardship for their own financial benefit. He gives this brilliant insight: Christ did not tell the rich young ruler or the disciples to give to His ministry. They had to "leave all" to follow Christ. They did not take their assets with them or give them to Christ. The rich young ruler was commanded to "give all" to the poor and not to Christ. The disciples did not provide Christ with their wealth as part of following Him. Jesus does not need money from manipulation or unethical means. Abundant financing always follows true stewardship. The disciples did not have to give Christ their wealth as part of following Him.

24. Craig Hill, *Wealth, Riches, and Money* (Littleton, CO: Family Foundations International, 2001), 232.

25. Ibid.

26. Alcorn, 26-27.

27. Mary Baker, "You Are God. There Is No Other" in *Reign*, 2014. Available on iTunes and www.MaryBakerMusic.com.

Heaven Invading: Raises

Before my wife and I got married, we developed a five-year plan. The goal was to be debt free—with exception of a mortgage—and maintain a lifestyle where solely my job could support us. It was important to us for Danielle to stay home with our children.

Three years into our marriage we were not very far along on our 5-year plan. We still had over $70,000 in student loans and car payments. Then I got fired. I was given two months' severance and ended up getting unemployment as well. The very next day, I recommitted my life to Christ and called my church to schedule my baptism, which I had been feeling the tug of God to do for quite a while.

During my hiatus from work, I made it my full-time job to find another one. A recruiter called me and I was offered the job as a contractor! I could do this job 100% remotely and work from home, so there was no need to relocate! Even more, it was a $20,000 pay raise from my previous job. Praise Jesus!

I loved the new job and put the newfound income to good use: paying down our car loans. We paid off both of our cars ten months later. My contract was renewed every three months, so I began looking for a permanent position. We sought prayer at church and one man prayed for a doubling of our income, which I honestly thought was a bit of a stretch.

A friend in our church passed on my résumé to a consulting firm he had just hired. They liked my résumé and I could feel God's favor in the interviews. I continued my prayers for God to give me the correct words to say and for my words to carry weight, which really paid off during salary negotiations. When discussing salary, I didn't feel the need to clarify the 'thousands' factor, and just used the number in front of the thousands separator comma. My interviewer took this to mean 'dollars-per-hour' as an hourly rate. The result was that I was paid double what I thought I was negotiating.

As it so happened, we were able to pay off our final student loan just one week before we left for our five-year anniversary trip to Hawaii—another blessing God granted us through His amazing provision. In total, we paid off about $40,000 of student loan debt in 5 months, with plenty left over to pad our savings account and take an amazing trip. God is a planner and we know that He gave us our five-year goals and provided a way to make them become a reality.

Caleb and Danielle

CHAPTER 7

Killing Sacred Cows Part 1: Jesus Was Poor

There was a farmer who had a cow with a wooden leg. A man driving by saw the cow and was so shocked that he stopped his car and asked the farmer about the cow. The farmer said that this was a special cow. He told stories of how the cow saved him and his kids' lives more than once. The driver was impressed, but that still didn't explain why the cow had a wooden leg. Finally, the farmer explained, "You can't eat a special cow like that all at once!" [1]

Religion has its own "sacred cows"—wrong beliefs that are kept alive no matter the cost. Sacred cows are protected from the butcher, even when people are starving. There really isn't a gentle way to kill a sacred cow. And, unlike the farmer's cow, sacred cows cannot be done away with gradually. You just need to kill them and deal with the fallout.

The Word of God is powerful and effective (Hebrews 4:12), it will not return void (Isaiah 55:11), and when mixed with faith—it will produce a miracle (Hebrews 4:2). So what's the problem? I believe one of the main problems is summarized by what Jesus said to the scribes and Pharisees, that they were "making the word of God of no effect through your tradition" (Mark 7:13 NKJV). Wrong teaching—specifically religious doctrines—nullifies the power of the Word of God, and makes it of no effect. [2]

When it comes to finances, there are some sacred cows that are making the Word of God of no effect. Jesus is the wisdom of God—the answer for every issue of life—including finances. He is our ultimate example of the life available through Him in the Kingdom. So, we will need to see what example Jesus set with finances.

I went through the Internet and looked at the biggest objections that people have (usually preachers) to God wanting to prosper His people. I have arranged this chapter and the next one around those questions and objections. Let's kill some sacred cows of financial blessing.

"Wrong teaching—specifically religious doctrines—nullifies the power of the Word of God and makes it of no effect."

SACRED COW: JESUS WAS POOR #1
"We are supposed to be like Jesus and Jesus was poor."

Have you heard this one? Was Jesus really poor?

Jesus did have money. He even had one of His disciples, Judas, designated to be the treasurer. I am going to make this simple: you only need a treasurer if you have treasure. I personally do not have enough money (yet) that I have to have somebody designated to look after it.

Do you remember the Last Supper? Jesus whispered in Judas' ear and he left to go out at night. What did the other disciples think Judas was doing? They thought, "Jesus is having Judas give to the poor again."[3] For them to assume this would mean that He had given to the poor before—maybe on a regular basis. In addition, there was so much money in the treasury the other disciples didn't even recognize Judas was stealing money for himself out of the moneybag.[4]

Jesus had enough money to support twelve disciples for three and a half years of ministry and still be an outrageous giver. Many scholars believe the disciples were teenagers—and you know how much teenage boys eat! Plus, there were times they had extended travelers with them.

How did Jesus have money? Here's the quick answer: His Dad provided it for Him (Who is the same Source and good Daddy to us as well—what a coincidence!).

Magi (wise men) from the East brought Him gifts to His house when He was an infant. Don't think about the Christmas card where the three shepherds and the three wise men were all there at the same time. The shepherds were there at Jesus' birth.[5] The wise men visited Jesus in His house when He was around two years old. [6] The Bible never says only three wise men came; we are only told that there were three gifts.

We need to understand who these Magi were. They were a group of people from the court of the Persian ruler. Part of their role was to promote the honor of the king of Persia, whose official title was "King of Kings." [7] The ruling body in the Parthian-Persian empire at this time was much like the Roman senate: they were the king-makers of the day and were composed entirely of Magi. [8] They were trained to identify and honor kingship. These king-makers traveled fifteen hundred miles from Persia to Jerusalem, a long, dangerous, and perilous journey into a foreign land because they recognized there was a superior King.

You would never see royal officials of that day, travel fifteen hundred miles carrying treasure chests by themselves. They traveled in a large convoy to the point that we read, "When Herod the King heard that the Magi from the East had come to Jerusalem, he was troubled ["deeply disturbed"] and all Jerusalem with him" (Matthew 2:3). Why would King Herod be freaking out if just three guys came from the East with their little knickknacks and said, "Here you go, Jesus!"? If that's what happened, why was all of Jerusalem in a stir?

It is absurd to think that these three wealthy sages traveled months to bring Jesus a few trinkets.

And [the wise men] fell down and worshiped [Jesus]. Then opening their treasures, they offered Him gifts, gold and frankincense and myrrh (Matthew 2:11).

The picture here is of opening their treasure chests to give Jesus gifts. [9] You can't help but remember when the Queen of Sheba came with her gifts of "gold and a great quantity of spices" to the son of David in Jerusalem. [10]

"Jesus wasn't poor."

Here is how the poverty spirit would have you picture the scene:

Three dusty men with big hats get off of their worn out donkeys, finally arriving at Jesus' house. One pulls out a little Ziploc baggie, "Here you go, Jesus. Here's this little gold nugget wrapped in tin foil." The other two reach into their pockets, "Here are some economy sizes we got from Wal-Mart. Use it sparingly." [11]

A small chest of gold measuring less than eight square inches would weigh over fifty pounds. That is over $1 million dollars today.[12] That is if it is a small chest. The other two gifts were extremely valuable as well. Even by conservative estimates, this offering would have been in the millions of dollars.

Right after that, Joseph is warned in a dream to flee to Egypt because Herod was going to try to kill Jesus.[13] They fled to Egypt where it is likely Egyptians wouldn't hire the Jews—and Jesus and His family were able to live for years in Egypt without any income!

Jesus wasn't poor.

SACRED COW: JESUS WAS POOR #2

"Jesus was poor. Joseph and Mary were poor. They had to offer a turtle dove at the temple for taxes."

The Law of Moses required that a purification offering be brought after a child was born.[14] If the parents could not afford a one-year-old lamb, they could offer two turtle doves or two pigeons, which is what Mary and Joseph offered.[15] Doesn't this prove they were poor?

It might except this occurred when Jesus was a baby. The Magi didn't come until Jesus was around two years old. After the Magi came, they weren't poor.

SACRED COW: JESUS WAS POOR #3

"The Bible says that Jesus became poor."

As we get ready to read 2 Corinthians 8:9, remember the context. All of 2 Corinthians 8 and 9 are speaking about finances and giving—two whole chapters about money![16]

> *For you know the grace of our Lord Jesus Christ, that though He was rich, yet for your sake He became poor, so that you by His poverty might become rich* (2 Corinthians 8:9).

Go back and read that verse again slowly. Here is the question we need to ask: in what sense did Jesus "become poor"?[17]

Was Jesus sick for all thirty-three years of His earthly life? No, yet,

Jesus "bore our sickness and carried our pain" (Isaiah 53:4). When did that happen? It happened on the Cross and in the beatings.

Was Jesus cursed by God for thirty-three years of His earthly life? No, yet, "Christ redeemed us from the curse of the law by becoming a curse for us—for it is written, 'Cursed is everyone who hanged on a tree'" (Galatians 3:13). So, when did Jesus become cursed? On the Cross, when He hung on a tree.

Was Jesus in sin for thirty-three years of His earthly life? No. "For our sake, He made Him to be sin who knew no sin so that in Him, we might become the righteousness of God" (2 Corinthians 5:21). When did Jesus become sin? On the Cross.

Was Jesus poor for thirty-three years of His earthly life? No. Read again 2 Corinthians 8:9 in light of what we just discussed, "For you know the grace of our Lord Jesus Christ, that though He was rich, yet for your sake He became poor, so that you by His poverty might become rich." When did Jesus become poor?[18] Here's what I believe this verse teaches: He took our poverty on the Cross, because as we already saw, He wasn't poor.

So, when did Jesus become poor? I would say the same time He became sick, the same time He became sin, the same time He became cursed. Jesus became poor at the Cross. It is inaccurate to say that Jesus was poor on earth and that we should follow His example of poverty.

Some of you are having a real struggle believing this because of all the "doctrines of men that make the word of God of no effect." If what I am saying is true, wouldn't that be good news? I encourage you to be like the Bereans, who "eagerly" searched the scriptures to see if what Paul said was true.[19]

Sin, sickness, the curse of the Law, demonic torment, poverty—they were not part of God's original creation. They are all a result of the Fall of man. Jesus lived free from all of this bondage in His earthly life and purchased our freedom in each of these areas through His death, burial, and resurrection.[20] These things were never God's will for His people.

Matthew 1:21 "You shall call His name Jesus, for He will save His people from their sins." Here's an American religious interpretation of that, "Jesus died for my sins. That means if I say the sinner's prayer, I will go to heaven when I die." Matthew is teaching that Jesus will save His people from every effect of sin. The book of Matthew was written to Jews, who thought differently than Americans. They saw sin as having a holistic affect on a person's life, not just their "spiritual" life. Take a few minutes right now and read Deuteronomy 28:1-14, you will see that obedience to God under the Old Covenant brought blessings to your life in the areas of favor, finances, fertility, protection, reputation, health,[21] long life,[22] angelic protection, etc.[23]

Aside from all of the specific blessings mentioned, here are some "summary statements" from Deuteronomy 28:

- "All these blessings shall come upon you and overtake you…" (verse 2).
- "Blessed shall you be when you come in, and blessed shall you be when you go out" (verse 6).
- "The Lord will command a blessing on you…" (verse 8).
- "…the Lord will make you abound in prosperity" (verse 11).
- "And you shall lend to many nations, but you shall not borrow. And the Lord will make you the head and not the tail, and you shall only go up and not down" (verses 12-13).

We now have a New and better Covenant with better promises![24] It is *biblically irresponsible* to say that God only paid for the forgiveness of sins on the Cross. Jews thought about sin more holistically than that. Michael L. Brown, a premier Hebrew scholar, summarizes the work of the Messiah as, "The whole man has been wholly healed."[25]

Let's say someone was drowning in an ocean and you come upon them. You wouldn't say, "I just want to save the person on the inside, because that's what's really important. I don't want to save your wallet or your clothes, those aren't important. So, if you could take those off first…" No! You pull out the whole person who is in a mess, and you save them. This is exactly the picture behind the word "redemption." God reached down into our mess and pulled us up and made His life in the Kingdom available to us. This is how most people view salvation: "God died for the forgiveness of your sins, but healing, financial prosperity, emotional health, those are separate issues." No, He died for the whole thing. Now, you receive these blessings by grace through faith, but He paid for the whole package at one time.

SACRED COW: JESUS WAS POOR #4
"When the Bible says that Jesus became poor so we could become rich, it was talking about spiritual riches."

Let's look at this verse again and ask, "Why did Jesus become poor?"

For you know the grace of our Lord Jesus Christ, that though He was rich, yet for your sake He became poor, so that you by His poverty might become rich (2 Corinthians 8:9).

Here's the reason Jesus became poor: so that you, by His poverty, might become rich. Jesus became poor for the same reason He bore our sickness and pain, became sin, became cursed—to set you free from the result of the Fall so you could experience the "abundant life" of His Kingdom.

Some people have tried to spiritualize this verse and say it only applies to Jesus becoming spiritually poor so we could become spiritually rich. Here's the problem with that thinking: the whole context of 2 Corinthians 8-9 is talking about money. The Greek word used here for "rich" speaks about material wealth in every other instance it is used in the New Testament. [26]

At the Cross, Jesus got what we deserved—every result of the Fall—so we could get what He deserved. It's not fair; it's grace! Let's look at some blessings (some we've already mentioned):

- Jesus became sin, so that you could become the righteousness of God. [27]
- Jesus carried our sickness and pain so that by His stripes we could be healed. [28]
- Jesus became cursed from the Law so that we could be redeemed from the curse and walk in covenant blessings. [29]
- Jesus became poor so that you might become rich. [30]
- Jesus is the One who will heal us emotionally. He "heals the brokenhearted." [31]
- Jesus "sets the captive free"—freedom from addictions. [32]
- Jesus delivers people from depression; He gives "the oil of gladness instead of mourning." [33]
- Jesus sets people free from deception; He "brings those from darkness to light." [34]
- Jesus frees people from demonic bondage and torment, "...that they may turn from darkness to light and from the power of satan to God." [35]

Some verses just paint a picture of Jesus paying for it all:

"God no more desires for you to be poor and in debt than He does for you to be in sin."

Grace to you and peace from God our Father and the Lord Jesus Christ, Who gave Himself for our sins to <u>deliver</u> <u>us</u> <u>from</u> <u>the</u> <u>present</u> <u>evil</u> <u>age</u>, according to the will of our God and Father... (Galatians 1:3-4).

Notice, it didn't say that Jesus came to deliver us and we would get to enjoy it in the sweet by and by. "When we all get to heaven, what a day of rejoicing that will be..." Yes, heaven will be better than we can imagine. But there can be freedom and rejoicing in the "rough now and now":

The reason the Son of God appeared was to destroy the works of the devil (1 John 3:8).

Jesus came to defeat the devil, expose his works, and reverse their effects.

Is poverty and lack from God, or of the devil? There are two job descriptions in the Bible (let's not confuse them): "I have come that you may have life," and "steal, kill and destroy" (John 10:10). Or, to make it simpler: God is good. Devil is bad. Abundance, prosperity, more than enough to be generous is characteristic of a good God. Poverty, lack, debt is the bad news of the devil.

Do you remember how Jesus taught His disciples to pray? "Your Kingdom come, Your will be done on earth as it is in heaven" (Matthew 6:10). Heaven is our model for life and ministry. Heaven is where God's will is perfectly done. Is there any poverty, sickness, sin or torment up in heaven? No, because that is not what God's will is. Jesus focused His followers' prayers to partner with God to make "up there" come "down here."

When Adam and Eve took their first breath, did they awake to an abundant garden with plenty? Or thorns, thistles, and hunger? When God took Israel into the Promised Land, was it flowing with milk and honey (a picture of abundant provision), or blowing with dust bunnies and tumbleweeds?

Prosperity is part of the atonement. In other words, Jesus paid for your abundant provision in the same way and to the same extent that He paid for the forgiveness of your sins and the healing of your body. God no more desires for you to be poor and in debt than He does for you to be in sin. If you are poor or in debt, this is not a time to feel condemnation; it is an invitation to experience more of what Jesus paid for.

What if one of my sons was sacrificed so that you could be free from sin, sickness, and poverty? What if you said, "I am just going to take the forgiveness of sins" and went on and lived in sickness and poverty? I would NOT think, "What a wonderful, humble person. They are so spiritual. They have chosen what is better." I would be angry and grieved. I would want you to walk in the fullness of what I paid for because such a high price was paid.

Let these words wash over you and remind you of God's heart for you in every situation:

> *He who did not spare His own Son but gave Him up for us all, how will He not also with Him graciously give us **all things*** (Romans 8:32)?

> *Without hesitation God abandoned His Son to death for the redemption of mankind; this grace gift is <u>all</u>-inclusive. This leaves us without any excuse to feel neglected or in lack* (Romans 8:32 The Mirror).[36]

> *If God didn't hesitate to put <u>everything</u> on the line for us, embracing our condition and exposing Himself to the worst by sending His own Son, is there <u>anything</u> else He wouldn't <u>gladly</u> <u>and</u> <u>freely</u> do for us* (Romans 8:32 MSG)?

SACRED COW: JESUS WAS POOR #5
"Jesus was homeless."

This isn't the weightiest issue in the Bible; however, if Jesus was a homeless beggar, then maybe we should try to emulate Him by becoming monks and taking vows of poverty. (Of course, we'd have to find someone who is not in poverty to support the monks to eat, live in the monastery, and not work.)

First of all, Jesus had a house in Capernaum:

And when He returned to Capernaum after some days, it was reported that He was at home (Mark 2:1).

[After Jesus appointed the 12 apostles] *Then He went home, and the crowd gathered again…* (Mark 3:20).

These verses clearly state that Jesus had a home or a house (same word in the Greek). Does any more really need to be said? Of course He could have sold it when He went out into traveling ministry. Some scholars believe He may have even kept the house in Capernaum even when He travelled for 3½ years for public ministry because Matthew just refers to it as "the house" in many places. [37]

It just doesn't make a lot of sense to think Jesus was homeless when you look at other verses:

"And leaving Nazareth He went and lived in Capernaum…" (Matthew 4:13). It is silly to think that Jesus was homeless in Nazareth and moved to homelessness in Capernaum.

Jesus was a carpenter. Where did He build things? Where did He keep His tools? Are we really supposed to believe He built things on the streets where He was living?

"Hold on, didn't Jesus say, 'the Son of Man has no place to lay His head'? See, He was homeless."

Jesus did say, "Foxes have holes, and birds of the air have nests, but the Son of Man has nowhere to lay His head" (Matthew 8:20). The context of this verse is *not* Jesus saying, "I'm so poor, I don't even have a place to sleep." The context is Jesus warning someone who wanted to be His follower that there was a cost. He follows up that statement with another one about priorities:

> *Another of the disciples said to Him, "Lord, let me first go and bury my father." And Jesus said to him, "Follow Me, and leave the dead to bury their own dead"* (Matthew 8:21-22).

When Jesus moved into itinerant ministry, He may not have had a house and some of the things people want for security, *but it wasn't because He couldn't afford it; it was because of His lifestyle of radical trust.* It is similar to a person who is a missionary and travels all of the time; they don't have their own home because it doesn't make sense for them to.

So, was Jesus poor? No. Jesus fits the definition of financial authority I laid out at the beginning:

> God not only desires to deliver you from financial bondage [Jesus never needed this part, but many of us do], but to position you into financial authority to where you are empowered to fulfill every divine assignment and help others fulfill theirs. [38]

INNER ACTION

1. In Mark 11:23 Jesus states:

    Truly, I say to you, whoever says to this mountain, "Be taken up and thrown into the sea," <u>and</u> <u>does</u> <u>not</u> <u>doubt</u> in his heart, but <u>believes</u> that what he says will come to pass, it will be done for him.

    Faith and doubt are like a team of horses hitched to each other and pulling in opposite directions. Faith will pull you towards the promise; doubt will pull you away from it. When doubt and faith are mixed together, they do not produce the power of God to change things. Removing doubt is like cutting the hitch that ties the horses together. When we do this, we can confidently expect God to renew our minds, change our hearts, and fulfill His Word in our life.

    It doesn't take a lot of faith to see a mountain move—only a mustard seed size faith—if you don't have any doubts. The sacred cows we have been slaying are doubts. If you have a 1% doubt that Jesus was prosperous, you will focus on that 1% and ignore the other 99%.

    As honestly as you can, where do you see yourself on the scale?

    Jesus was poor | | | Jesus was prosperous

2. Being as candid as possible, what would you say you really believe about the abundant provision and generosity that Jesus lived? What can you expect, as a child of God?

Endnotes

1. Story adapted from a teaching article by Andrew Wommack, "Killing Sacred Cows." Accessed at http://www.awmi.net/extra/article/sacred_cows July 23, 2014.

2. Ibid.

3. John 13:29

4. John 12:6

5. Luke 2:8-21.

6. Matthew 2:1-12. It is likely that Jesus was up to 2 years old when the Magi visited. First, they went to a house (Matthew 2:11), not a barn or a stable. Second, it uses the word "child" (Matthew 2:11) which is translated from the Greek word *paidion*, which can mean infant, but also means "young child." There is a different Greek word for a "newborn"—*brephos*—that was used in Luke when describing the infant Jesus. Herod went and ordered the killing of the male children in Bethlehem that were two years old and younger.

7. Craig S. Keener, *A Commentary on the Gospel of Matthew* (Grand Rapids: Eerdmans, 1999), 99.

8. John MacArthur, *The MacArthur New Testament Commentary Matthew 1-7* (Chicago: Moody Press, 1985), 31.

9. Grant R. Osbourne, *Matthew* in Exegetical Commentary on the New Testament (Grand Rapids: Zondervan, 2010), 91.

10. 1 Kings 10:1-10.

11. Dr. Mike Brown described that scene with similar language in his excellent message "Financial Authority" available at www.StrengthandWisdomMinistries.com.

12. 50 pounds = 800 ounces x price of gold/ounce at the time of this writing ($1310.10) = $1,040,880.

13. Matthew 2:13-15.

14. Leviticus 12:8.

15. Luke 2:22-24.

16. In 2 Corinthians 8-9, Paul is giving them instructions on having the offering

ready when he comes, mostly for the poor in Jerusalem.

17. It could be that compared to the riches He had in heaven, He was poor. In other words, His being "poor" was relative. This could be what the verse means, but I think it is something else.

18. We already saw that He had a treasure box given to Him at His birth by the king-makers of the day, so He was not poor His entire life on earth.

19. Acts 17:11. There is a big difference between a "noble Berean" and a "negative brother." The Bereans were noble because they heard the Good News Paul was preaching and eagerly searched the scriptures to confirm it. Many today think they are acting like noble Bereans, but they are actually just negative brothers (and sisters). They already have their mind made up what the Bible says and they will find verses to support it. They are very argumentative. They appoint themselves as watchdogs in the body of Christ and love to blast people publicly, especially online, whom they have never met with, corresponded with, or sat under their ministry. I see them as the modern day Pharisees that followed Paul's ministry and put people into bondage.

20. 1 John 3:8.

21. "Health" is not mentioned in Deuteronomy 28 as a blessing, but it is clearly stated as part of the Old Covenant blessings: Exodus 15:26; 23:25, 26.

22. Exodus 20:12; 23:26.

23. Psalm 91.

24. Hebrews 8:6. If you read Deuteronomy 28:15-68, you will see the consequences for sin were just as holistic as the blessings.

25. Michael L. Brown, *Israel's Divine Healer* (Grand Rapids: Zondervan, 1995), 198.

26. The Greek word for "rich" is *plousios*. It is used 28 times in the New Testament and always refers to material riches, unless it is accompanied by the preposition *en*, which is translated "in"; then it is figurative in use; this only occurs twice in the New Testament: Ephesians 2:4, "But God, being *rich in* mercy..." James 2:5, "...to be *rich in* faith." The reference in 2 Corinthians 9:8 is not accompanied by the preposition *en* and is not figurative in use.

27. 2 Corinthians 5:21.

28. Isaiah 53:4, 5 with Matthew 8:16, 17.

29. Galatians 3:13.

30. 2 Corinthians 8:9

31. Isaiah 61:1.

32. Luke 4:18.

33. Isaiah 61:3.

34. Colossians 1:13.

35. Acts 26:18.

36. A paraphrase from the original Greek Text by Francois du Toit (Hermanus, South Africa : Mirror Word Publishing, 2012).

37. Matthew 4:13; 9:28; 13:1, 36; 17:25. Grant R. Osbourne, *Matthew* in Exegetical Commentary on the New Testament (Grand Rapids: Zondervan, 2010), 305.

38. Mike Brown's definition of "financial authority" from his sermon CD, "Financial Authority" available at www.StrengthandWisdomMinistries.com.

Heaven Invading: Debt Cancelled

My husband was working as an executive and owner for a commercial real estate company and we were developing a residential condo property in Florida. We had taken out a $3 Million loan with a large bank and had personally guaranteed the loan. When the project was about 1/2 completed and sold off, the real estate market fell out in Florida. For the next 2 years, we did everything we could to complete and sell off the remaining project but nothing was moving! And we still owed the bank $1.5 Million! They continuously demanded their money!

It was a tremendous amount of stress for both of us. Although we did our best to avoid it, this debt influenced every area of our lives in a negative way. We did everything we could to work with the bank, and they did everything they could to get us to pay. At one point, Ron suggested what is called, a deed in lieu of foreclosure. Basically, the bank takes over ownership of the property, and we are released from the debt. Everyone involved laughed and said, "Why would the bank ever do that!?"

We started searching the Scriptures and receiving more truth on finances and debt and we knew this was NOT God's heart. Once you know His heart, you can start praying in line with His will. One night, Ron and his prayer buddies were in our home praying. Ron fell to his knees and told the Lord, "Father, it's in your hands." He shared his experience with the guys and said, "I am handing it over to the Father. It is His." Later that night, he shared his experience with me saying, "...something broke tonight in the Spirit realm."

The next day, the same Holy Spirit power descended on me, and I fell to my knees. I called Ron at work and shared the news with him.

THAT AFTERNOON, out of nowhere, the bank called and offered Ron a deed in lieu of foreclosure!! No questions asked, no reason why, they just said, "You can walk away!" $1.5 Million GONE, just like that. We should have lost everything.

Ron and Kristen

CHAPTER 8

Killing Sacred Cows Part 2: Financial Prosperity Is Not God's Will For Me

The price of beef may have gone down from the surplus of cows killed from the last chapter. Put on your butcher's apron and gloves and pick out your favorite marinade—we have still got a ways to go.

SACRED COW: PROSPERITY IS NOT GOD'S WILL FOR ME #1
"Hasn't there been bad teaching in the Church on finances and prosperity?"

Yes. There has also been bad teaching on heaven, but I still plan on going there. Many "prosperity" teachers partnered with the spirit of Mammon and twisted the Bible's teaching on finances to be man-centered instead of God-centered.

Imagine two ditches, both represent biblical error—one on each side of the road. One strategy of the enemy is to show you one ditch and to have you react to it so strongly that you end up swerving into the other ditch. Don't ignore the awesome truths and promises in the Bible about our abundant provision just because of the abuses of teaching by others.

SACRED COW: PROSPERITY IS NOT GOD'S WILL FOR ME #2
"You shouldn't be talking about money. There are more important things to talk about. You need to teach like Jesus."

Jesus had more to say about finances than just about any other topic—more than the second coming, faith, prayer, and hell combined. Fifteen percent of everything Jesus said in the Gospels dealt with money and possessions. So, if you want to teach like Jesus, you may want to start talking

---

"Money is a litmus test of where your heart is, who you are serving, and what you really believe about God."

---

about money.

Why did Jesus put such an emphasis on money? Jesus recognized that money is a spiritual indicator of what is going on in your heart. It's a litmus test of where your heart is, who you are serving, and what you *really* believe about God. *"Do I really believe He's good? Do I really believe He's trustworthy?"* Again, you can confess, sing, dance, Jericho march, and blow the shofar (all good in their place), but your heart is revealed by the way you treat money.

It's interesting: Jesus linked money with salvation. Do you remember the story of Zacchaeus, who was a chief tax collector?[1] Tax collectors were hated in Israel because they extorted money from the Jews as they collected taxes for the Romans.[2] When Zacchaeus said he would give half of his money to the poor and repay everybody four times what he stole from them, Jesus did not say, "Great idea. I am going to put that testimony in My newsletter." Jesus said, "Today, salvation has come to this house" (Luke 19:9). That is absolutely amazing. He didn't even raise his hand and say a prayer. Jesus saw a generous heart that gave cheerfully as a sign of salvation.

SACRED COW: PROSPERITY IS NOT GOD'S WILL FOR ME #3
"Seeking financial prosperity is selfish."

Some have turned the pursuit of prosperity into selfish ambition, but that is not what the Bible teaches. Biblical prosperity is not selfish (see Chapter One for more about how prosperity is not all about you, it is about being a blessing to others). From beginning to end, the Bible paints a picture of God blessing His children so they can be a blessing.

SACRED COW: PROSPERITY IS NOT GOD'S WILL FOR ME #4

"You should just preach the Gospel, not that 'Prosperity Gospel!'"

Jesus is in the synagogue and He stands up and reads the scroll from Isaiah 61:

> *"The Spirit of the Lord is upon Me, because He has anointed Me to* ***proclaim good news to the poor***. *He has sent Me to proclaim liberty to the captives and recovering of sight to the blind, to set at liberty those who are oppressed, to proclaim the year of the Lord's favor." And He rolled up the scroll and gave it back to the attendant and sat down. And the eyes of all in the synagogue were fixed on Him. And He began to say to them, "Today this Scripture has been fulfilled in your hearing"* (Luke 4:18-21).

There are negative conditions that are named with solutions the Messiah would bring:

- Captives—receive liberty
- Blind—recovery of sight
- Oppressed—set free

What was the solution to the poor? That the Good News, the Gospel is preached to them. Jesus repeats this thought to John the Baptist's disciples:

> *Now when John heard in prison about the deeds of the Christ, he sent word by his disciples and said to Him, "Are you the one who is to come, or shall we look for another?" And Jesus answered them, "Go and tell John what you hear and see: the blind receive their sight and the lame walk, lepers are cleansed and the deaf hear, and the dead are raised up, and* ***the poor have good news preached to them***" (Matthew 11:2-5).

Again, there are negative conditions that are named with solutions the Messiah would bring:

- Blind—receive their sight
- Lame—walk
- Lepers—cleansed

- Deaf—hear
- Dead—raised up
- Poor—have the Good News preached to them

What is going on here? How is the Good News, the Gospel being preached, the answer and remedy to poverty?

When the Gospel is preached, it contains the power of God,[3] and there is a supernatural lifeline to pull someone out of sin, sickness, death, and yes—poverty! There is no "Prosperity Gospel"—only the Gospel of Jesus Christ that contains in it the solution for everything afflicting humanity as a result of sin. Good News to a poor man is that he doesn't have to be poor any more!

Don't hear what I am not saying. I am not saying that you are in sin if you are poor. I am not saying that you are righteous if you are wealthy. I am saying that part of the provision of the Cross was that you have more than enough to meet your needs and to be generous to meet the needs of others. I'm not talking about everyone being a millionaire. Your wealth will be in proportion to your calling, stewardship, season, and faith.

SACRED COW: PROSPERITY IS NOT GOD'S WILL FOR ME #5
"Jesus said, 'The poor you will always have among you.'"

Unfortunately, not everyone will take hold of everything Jesus paid for. There will always be sick people and sinners among us. That doesn't mean that sickness and sin are His will or that He didn't pay for them to be free of that. It is the same with poverty. Just because someone doesn't take a hold of everything He paid for, it doesn't mean He didn't pay for it.

"One of the poorest ways to help the poor is to be poor."

SACRED COW: PROSPERITY IS NOT GOD'S WILL FOR ME #6
"It's more spiritual to be poor."

In order for you to be a steward, you have to have something to steward. The Bible is full of commands to help the poor. One of the poorest ways to help the poor is to be poor. The Bible is full of commands to be generous. How are you going to be generous if you don't have enough to give? Read this paragraph again and let it sink in. [4]

Believing that it is spiritual to be poor is one of the most dangerous deceptions among Christians today. Some people are so religious that if an angel came down from the throne of God and gave them money, they would think they had to quickly give it all away because they believe that God doesn't want you to have anything. That doesn't necessarily please God. If He tells you to give it all away, give it all away. If He says keep it, do it. God is the Owner; I am His money manager. For some people, it is easier to give money away than to be a good steward of it.

Throughout history, the church perpetrates the devaluing of blessing. There has been this idea that if you are poor and broke all of the time then you were dependent on the Lord.

In a sermon, Bill Johnson asked:

What would you rather have: food supernaturally appearing every day? Or to have a successful job where you prosper? That is the difference between the wilderness and the Promised Land. The Promised Land was not supernatural provision every day. The Promised Land was God blessing their work.

There are many people who look at the lifestyle of daily dependence as the goal to be obtained, but it is actually the school. You don't live in school; unless you aren't very good at it and you are required to repeat a grade over and over. The process is not where you live; it is what you go through to get where God has designed you to be.

Why do you think Jesus had His disciples leave everything? But when He left He made sure they had a sword and a coat—they had things that they couldn't have during the journey. The time without basic possessions taught them the proper stewardship principles so they could possess and possess correctly. [5]

Paul didn't tell Timothy to rebuke the rich or have them give away all of their money. Instead, he warned them to keep their trust in the Lord and not in their riches.

As for the rich in this present age, charge them not to be haughty, nor to set their hopes on the uncertainty of riches, but on <u>God, who richly provides us with everything to enjoy</u> (1 Timothy 6:17).

What kind of a reflection is it on our Dad when we act like He is Ebenezer Scrooge—a miser fretting over every penny? What kind of a parent wants their child to barely scrape by? To own nothing? To be in the bondage of debt? What would you think of a dad who had money but said, "I don't care if you have blisters on your feet, you can wear those shoes a little bit more. This honors me as your father to show how little you can live on."

I enjoy my kids having nice things. I enjoy watching them smile and laugh and have a good time. I'm not talking about excess; I'm not talking about greed; I'm talking about being a good dad.

You parents—if your children ask for a loaf of bread, do you give them a stone instead? Or if they ask for a fish, do you give them a snake? Of course not! So if you sinful people know how to give good gifts to your children, <u>how much more will your heavenly Father give good gifts</u> to those who ask Him (Matthew 7:9-11 NLT).

Israel took up three tithes: an annual tithe for the Levites and priests, an annual tithe for the feasts, and a tithe every three years for the poor.[6] The annual tithe for the feasts was basically so that Israel could go party at the festivals. It was to remind them of the goodness of God and the life He gave them to enjoy.

God gives us wealth to enjoy money, relationships, and prosperity of soul. It's not just about money, but it includes money.

Fear not, little flock, for it is your Father's good <u>pleasure</u> to give you the kingdom (Luke 12:32).

Let the Lord be magnified, Who has <u>pleasure in the prosperity</u> of His servant (Psalm 35:27 NKJV).

…go after God, who piles on all the riches we could ever manage (1 Timothy 6:17 MSG).

Poverty is not spiritual. Enjoying God's blessings is spiritual. God has called us to stewardship—NOT poverty!

SACRED COW: PROSPERITY IS NOT GOD'S WILL FOR ME #7
"Didn't Jesus say that the rich are evil and the poor are good?"

No, He did not.

If money is so bad for us, why doesn't satan just pour money on Christians? The more money, the quicker they would backslide. If money is so bad, why did satan take it away from Job? Why at the end of the book did God reward Job with a double portion? [7]

SACRED COW: PROSPERITY IS NOT GOD'S WILL FOR ME #8
"Jesus said, 'woe to the rich and blessed are the poor.'"

Blessed are you who are poor, for yours is the kingdom of God... But woe to you who are rich, for you have received your consolation (Luke 6:20, 24).

Let me ask you something: Is someone who is poor, who worships idols and sacrifices children really blessed just because they are poor? And is a person who loves and serves God and stewards great wealth for the Kingdom really cursed just for being rich?

You have to understand how Jesus taught. Jesus wasn't making a general statement that is true across all time. Jesus often taught by turning the tables on what was generally thought to be true in His day. [8] He would take the prevailing thought of His day and flip it on its head. It's like He would say, "Here is how you think it works, but it is actually the opposite in My Kingdom."

For example, in Luke 14, people thought the way to climb the social ladder was to take a seat by the head table. Jesus showed that in the Kingdom, those who humble themselves will be exalted. In the parable of the Great Banquet people would only invite to dinner those who could pay them back. Jesus said to use hospitality to invite the poor, crippled, lame, and the blind—those who cannot repay—and they would be rewarded in heaven.

So, when Jesus says, "Woe to you who are rich," Jesus is giving people a completely different view of reality. Everyone thought that the rich "had it made." Jesus is showing the reversal of the accepted:

- "Blessed are the poor, for yours is the Kingdom of God" (Luke 6:20).
- "Blessed are you who are hungry, for you shall be satisfied" (Luke 6:21).
- "Blessed are you who weep now, for you shall laugh" (Luke 6:21).
- "Blessed are you when people hate you" (Luke 6:22).

Jesus did not say, "Here are the requirements in order for you to be blessed: you must be poor, hungry, sad, and hated." He did not say, "It is a huge blessing to be poor, hungry, sad, and hated." The blessing is not in the condition; the blessing is that the Kingdom of God has now become available through Jesus to people nobody thought could be blessed (the poor, hungry, sad, hated). The people everybody thought were already blessed—the rich—are not the blessed ones. If all they have is their riches and are outside the Kingdom, they are cursed.

All of Israel was waiting for the day when somebody would say:

*The Spirit of the Lord is upon Me, because the Lord has anointed Me to bring good news to the **poor**. He has sent Me to bind up the **brokenhearted**...to comfort all who **mourn**...* (Isaiah 61:1, 2).

Who is bringing the Good News? The Lord's anointed, the Messiah.[9] You may remember when Jesus got up in His hometown to begin His public ministry; those are the words He read out of Isaiah 61. When He finished reading them, He said, "Today this Scripture is fulfilled in your hearing" (Luke 4:21). In other words, "It's me. I am the Lord's anointed. I am the Messiah."

When you look at who the Good News is coming to, it's kind of an odd bunch—"the poor, the brokenhearted, all who mourn." The Good News is expressing that now the Kingdom is coming to you. The Good News will be for poor people, brokenhearted people, and grieving people—the people who usually say, "*Not me. I missed out on the Good News. I am an outsider. I'm a little street kid sitting with his nose pressed up against the glass of the window at the restaurant looking at the lucky people eating inside. They get to feast at the table, not me.*"

And then the Lord's anointed, the Messiah will say, "No, no, no. It's you. All of you can come in now." This Good News is what the world was waiting for.[10]

If Jesus were speaking these Beatitudes today, Dallas Willard says they might sound like this:

- Blessed are the physically repulsive,
- Blessed are those who smell bad,
- The twisted, misshapen, deformed,
- The too big, too little, too loud,
- The bald, the fat, and the old—
- For they are all riotously celebrated in the party of Jesus.[11]

Dallas then moves on to the more serious outsiders saying blessed are:

The flunk-outs and drop-outs and burned-outs. The broke and the broken. The drug heads and the divorced. The HIV positive and herpes-ridden. The brain-damaged, the incurably ill. The barren and the pregnant many-times or at the wrong time. The over-employed, the underemployed, the unemployed. The unemployable. The swindled, shoved aside, the replaced. The parents with children living on the street, the children with parents not dying in the "rest" home. The lonely, the incompetent, the stupid. The emotionally starved or emotionally dead.[12]

This is Good News: regardless of bad genes, bad health, bad choices, or bad circumstances, you have not missed your chance. The Kingdom is here now, available through Jesus. You can begin now and know its fullness one day in eternity.

You may be thinking, "What about the people not in that category? What about the well-off and the well-fed, the happy and the well-spoken of?" Well, of course, the Kingdom is available to them too. It is available to everybody. But Jesus does give a warning in Luke 6 that we need to hear as well. Because people in that other category—the well-off, well-fed, happy, well-spoken of—can sometimes mistake the blessed life for the well-managed, well-financed, well-thought of, well-dressed, well-educated, well-off life.

Christians can start to think, *this is the life blessed by God; those are the lucky ones.* This is where entitlement, pride, and arrogance start to creep into the Jesus community. Often we are unaware of it, but it happens. And instead of being a welcoming family of Jesus lovers, they form a little club for elite people. And people who don't have a well-managed, well-financed, well-thought of, well-dressed life look at them and say, "I could never belong to that club."

Here is the message of the Kingdom: Everybody's welcome here. Nobody's perfect. Anything is possible.[13]

Who is really well off? Who is really blessed? Me. Not because I have it all together, but because Jesus came for me. Do you know who else is blessed? You. Not because you have abundant resources, education, and good looks. But because the Kingdom of God is available and through reliance on the Person of Jesus—you can live in that if you want to.

SACRED COW: PROSPERITY IS NOT GOD'S WILL FOR ME #9

"Didn't Jesus say that it's impossible for the rich to enter the Kingdom of God?"

No.

And Jesus said to His disciples, "Truly, I say to you, only with difficulty will a rich person enter the kingdom of heaven. Again I tell you, it is easier for a camel to go through the eye of a needle than for a rich person to enter the kingdom of God" (Matthew 19:23-24).

"If poverty is such a good thing, why does the Bible command us to take care of the poor?"

Jesus is saying rich people will have additional obstacles to overcome that poor people are not distracted by or encumbered with.

SACRED COW: PROSPERITY IS NOT GOD'S WILL FOR ME #10

"Humility is asking for no more than my needs to be met."

You may call it humility, but it is actually a selfish attitude. There is a whole world out there in need and all you care about is you and your family?

If poverty is such a good thing, why does the Bible command us to take care of the poor? Why would God have us interfere with the "humility" of the poor by giving to them?

Remember, one of the poorest ways to help the poor is to be poor! Church history has portrayed monks who take a vow of poverty and walk around in robes with a tin cup as a godly attitude. Here's the irony: those same monks who take a vow of poverty have to live off of the wealth of those who give to support their lifestyle.

"God did not provide prosperity so you can spend all of your wealth on yourself."

The true purpose of prosperity is so you can "abound unto every good work" (2 Corinthians 9:8); so you can have your needs met, but also meet the needs of others. God did not provide prosperity so you can spend all your wealth on yourself.

With that said, God doesn't mind you having your needs met in style. Remember: His name is *El Shaddai*, not *El Cheapo*. You don't have to see what the minimum amount you can survive on is and call that good stewardship. God doesn't mind you having nice things. God isn't broke. He doesn't mind you having money, but it is so you can be a blessing to others. Your true prosperity is not so you can spend it on yourself; it is so you can be a blessing, so you can be a giver, so you can fund the gospel reaching every nation, tribe, and tongue.

SACRED COW: PROSPERITY IS NOT GOD'S WILL FOR ME #11
"The 'Lord's Prayer' says that we should only ask for our 'daily bread.' That means we should only expect God to meet our basic needs."

Give us this day our daily bread (Matthew 6:11).

There is an expression some people use when it comes to finances, "I live by faith." We can picture a missionary saying that. What they mean is that they have no visible support or salary; they are dependent upon God to supply their needs, often through the generosity of others.

Here is the truth: all of us live by faith. This is right at the heart of "give us this day our daily bread" (Matthew 6:11). As you pray this prayer, you turn your eyes from the resource of provision (job, parents, investments) directly to the Source Himself—God who supplies your need using the resource of your job (or whatever else) to do it.

In this scenario, if you were to lose your job, you haven't lost your Source of supply. Your eyes always look beyond the resource to the Source. God is your supply. Today, you have God, and He has the provision. Tomorrow it will be the same because He never changes.

This is how children do it. If I discovered that my kids were saving up cereal, fruit, and bread because they were afraid of not having enough food to eat tomorrow, I would be shocked. It would hurt me that they didn't trust me enough to provide for them each day. It is okay to have possessions and provisions for tomorrow. What shuts down living in the Kingdom is trusting in them for future security. Our real security is in our loving Father who is with us every day.[14]

Trusting God doesn't mean we can just sit on the couch and watch soap operas all day and say, "God will supply my needs." I have met a number of people who quit their jobs and say, "I am waiting on God" when what they really mean is *"I am too lazy to work and I am counting on people in the church to love me too much to let me starve to death or be homeless. I am going to count on them to support me and call it 'living by faith.'"*

The church in Thessalonica had some of these, and Paul gave them instructions (read the underlined sentence for a powerful statement on the love of God):

> *Now we command you, brothers, in the name of our Lord Jesus Christ, that you keep away from any brother who is walking in idleness and not in accord with the tradition that you received from us. For you yourselves know how you ought to imitate us, because we were not idle when we were with you, nor did we eat anyone's bread without paying for it, but with toil and labor we worked night and day, that we might not be a burden to any of you. It was not because we do not have that right, but to give you in ourselves an example to imitate. For even when we were with you, we would give you this command: If anyone is not willing to work, let him not eat. For we hear that some among you walk in idleness, not busy at work, but busybodies. Now such persons we command and encourage in the Lord Jesus Christ to do their work quietly and to earn their own living* (2 Thessalonians 3:6-12).

SACRED COW: PROSPERITY IS NOT GOD'S WILL FOR ME #12
"The Bible says that godly people are to be content with what they have. That means we shouldn't seek to have more."

Have you ever seen those TV commercials for a prescription drug?

While they are showing the happy couple holding hands and walking on the beach, the voiceover is announcing all of the potentially dangerous side effects. For example (by the way, these are all real side effects):[15]

> Explosive diarrhea, amnesia, temporary paralysis, rainbow colored urine, impotence, hallucinations, night terrors, compulsive gambling, paranoia, suicidal ideation, disappearing fingerprints, lactation in men, rectal bleeding, excessive hair growth, psychosis, loss of bladder control, uncontrollable crying spells, uncontrollable rhyming and (last but not least)—premature death.

Wealth has some pretty powerful side effects as well. If you saw a commercial for wealth on TV, it would have some strong warnings of its own.[16] Paul gives a kind of "side effect" warning about wealth:

> *But godliness with contentment is great gain, for we brought nothing into the world, and we cannot take anything out of the world. But if we have food and clothing, with these we will be content. But those who desire to be rich fall into temptation, into a snare, into many senseless and harmful desires that plunge people into ruin and destruction. For the love of money is a root of all kinds of evils. It is through this craving that some have wandered away from the faith and pierced themselves with many pangs* (1 Timothy 6:6-12).

Let's summarize Paul's warnings:[17]
- Falling into temptation
- Falling into a snare
- Being controlled by senseless and harmful (habit-forming) desires
- Plunging headfirst into ruin
- Plunging headfirst into destruction
- Wandering from the faith
- Piercing with many pangs and grief

Paul names one antidote to all of these side effects: "contentment" (1 Timothy 6:6). Contentment is:

Learning to become sufficient in Christ's sufficiency and productive in present circumstances, conditions, seasons, or restrictions while still looking forward with expectation to God's next season and opportunity for their life.[18]

This passage of Scripture is *not* saying we can't have money. It is *not* saying a godly attitude means you can't have riches. Money is not the problem; it's peoples' attitude towards money that is the problem—"the love of money." It's the belief that money and true riches are the same thing.

Many people can't tell the difference between having riches and trusting in riches. When you love money and what it will produce more than you love God *there is a huge problem.* When you rely on money instead of looking to God as your Source *that is idolatry.*[19]

If riches were so bad and poverty was so good, you would think Paul would just tell the church to get rid of money as quickly as possible. Instead, just five verses later Paul gives additional "antidotes" to offset the effects of wealth:

> *As for the rich in this present age, charge them not to be haughty, nor to set their hopes on the uncertainty of riches, but on God, **who richly provides us with everything to enjoy.** They are to do good, to be rich in good works, to be generous and ready to share, thus storing up treasure for themselves as a good foundation for the future, so that they may take hold of that which is truly life* (1 Timothy 6:17-19).

- Avoid being haughty or arrogant
- Avoid putting your hope on the uncertainty of riches
- Put your hope in God
- Do good
- Be rich in good works
- Be generous and ready to share

Paul says that you can have wealth *and* contentment if your motive is right. It isn't anymore godly to be poor than it is godly to be rich. Money has nothing to do with godliness. You can be content with what you have and still desire more because you want to be a bigger blessing to others. The reason God blesses us is so we can be a blessing. Remember: real prosperity is defined by how much we give away—not by how much we keep for ourselves.

SACRED COW: PROSPERITY IS NOT GOD'S WILL FOR ME #13
"Is it God's will for me to prosper financially?"

Hopefully after these two chapters you believe the answer is "YES!"

I hope you began to personalize it. Now, take it out of the realm of doctrine, "Financial prosperity is God's will" and make it personal, "It is God's will for *me* to prosper financially."

> *And God is able to make **all** grace **abound** to you, so that having **all** sufficiency in **all** things at **all** times, you may **abound** in **every** good work* (2 Corinthians 9:8).

Are you noticing a pattern here? It doesn't really give the picture of God just wanting us to scrape by. Listen to the same verse in the Amplified Bible:

> *And God is able to make all grace (every favor and earthly blessing) come to you in abundance, so that you may always and under all circumstances and whatever the need be self-sufficient [possessing enough to require no aid or support and furnished in abundance for every good work and charitable donation]* (2 Corinthians 9:8 AMP).

The Lord gives us His grace, which produces financial prosperity, so we can then abound unto every good work. Either this verse is true or it's not true. **If this verse isn't true, then John 3:16 isn't true either.**

If we desire to give more but aren't able to because of financial lack, then we aren't fully prosperous in the way the Lord desires. I have good news: there is more grace we can learn to take hold of! True prosperity isn't measured in what we keep but in how much we are able to give. Prosperity is learning how to live out of the abundance of the Kingdom in every circumstance.

I am going take Mike Brown's definition of "financial authority" and personalize it. Read it and reread it. Let God's heart wash over you.

> God not only desires to deliver me from financial bondage [debt], but to position me into financial authority to where I am empowered to fulfill every divine assignment and help others fulfill theirs.[20]

SACRED COW: PROSPERITY IS NOT GOD'S WILL FOR ME #14
"Are you saying I am out of God's will if I am not prospering financially?"

Let me answer that question with a question. Have you sinned since you have been water baptized? I have. And yet, the Bible teaches that we died to sin when we were buried with Christ through baptism (Romans 6:1-14). So that tells me that there are things Jesus paid for that we as believers have not yet learned to fully take hold of. A believer sinning doesn't make the truth of being "dead to sin" any less true; it just means we are growing in our experience of what He paid for.

It is the same thing with His abundant provision. Jesus paid for us to "abound in every good work" (2 Corinthians 9:8). If we are not walking in the fullness of that yet, it becomes an invitation for us to experience more of Him and His promise.

Some people say, "Well, the most important thing is that people get saved." I agree. Jesus asked, "What will it profit a man if he gains the whole world and forfeits his soul?" (Matthew 16:26). However, it is neither humble nor spiritual to ignore the other aspects of the Cross. It is an insult.

If I paid a high price so you could be free from slavery, receive medical care, education, and food; I would not think you were noble or humble if you only went to school and still lived like a pauper in slavery. I paid for it all; it would bless me to see you take hold of all of it. Our heavenly Father has this same attitude:

He who did not spare His own Son but gave Him up for us all, how will He not also with Him graciously give us all things (Romans 8:32)?

INNER ACTION

Declarations are a way to demolish strongholds (2 Corinthians 10:4-5). It is a way to intentionally speak the truth to renew our minds to what God says is true. It is a way to think on purpose.

1.   Read the following declarations from Steve Backlund.[21] Mark next to each a number 1-10. One indicates it doesn't "feel" true. A 10 indicates that it feels true.

- In every area of my life, I live in abundance.
- I am blessed to be a blessing.
- I have more than enough to sow into the Kingdom of God.
- I make great financial decisions.
- The distribution of my wealth becomes the answer to the prayers of those in need.
- The favor of God weighs so heavily on my life that I am perpetually moving in the right direction to be a blessing to others.
- I have divine wisdom and insight when making decisions about my finances.
- The wealth that I accrue in my life will be a blessing to my children's children's children.
- God desires to prosper me financially.
- Whenever I have financial gain, I re-invest well and give generously.

2.   Post the above declarations somewhere you will see them every day or carry them around with you. Speak them out loud every day for a month and journal the changes in your thinking.

Endnotes

1. Luke 19:1-10

2. *Zondervan Illustrated Bible Backgrounds Commentary Vol. 1*, ed. Clinton E. Arnold (Grand Rapids: Zondervan, 2002), 463.

3. Romans 1:16, 17

4. Dallas Willard has an amazing chapter called "Is Poverty Spiritual?" in *Spirit of the Disciplines* (San Francisco: HarperSanFrancisco, 1988).

5. Bill Johnson, "Being Blessed Is Required" available at https://shop.ibethel.org/products/open-heavens-october 2010 complete set.

6. Number 18:21-25; Deuteronomy 14:22-27; Deuteronomy 14:28-29.

7. Job 42:10

8. Much of what follows here I learned from the teachings of Dallas Willard; especially the view of the Beatitudes as not the condition for the Kingdom, but people who it is now available to.

9. The word "Christ" is not Jesus' last name. It's a Greek word *khristos* from a little verb, *krio* which meant "to anoint." "Christ" means "the anointed one" or "the Messiah."

10. I heard John Ortberg tie the Isaiah 61:1-2 with the Beatitudes in a brilliant message called "How to Be Really Well Off."

11. Dallas Willard, *The Divine Conspiracy*, 123.

12. Ibid., 123-124

13. The section on the message to the "well-offs" was inspired by John Ortberg's message "How to Be Really Well Off."

14. Dallas Willard, *The Divine Conspiracy*, 261.

15. As reported in "10 Bizarre Side Effects to Common Medicines" at http://listverse.com/2011/02/03/10-bizarre-side-effects-to-common-medicines/ and "Top 10 Weirdest Prescription Drug Side Effects" at http://health.howstuffworks.com/medicine/medication/10-weird-prescription-drug-side-effect.htm both accessed on September 8, 2014.

16. I got the idea of wealth having side effects from Andy Stanley, *How To Be Rich*

(Grand Rapids: Zondervan, 2013), 55-56.

17. The idea for a warning of side effects from this passage is adapted from Stanley, 93.

18. Dr. Mike Brown sermon, "The Law of Contentment" available at www. StrengthandWisdom.com.

19. Andrew Wommack, *Financial Stewardship* (Tulsa, OK: Harrison House, 2012), 102-103.

20. Adapted from Mike Brown's definition of "financial authority" from his sermon CD, "Financial Authority" available at www.StrengthandWisdomMinistries. com.

21. Steve Backlund, *Declarations: Unlocking Your Future* (Igniting Hope Ministries, 2013), 78. Used with permission.

Heaven Invading: Blessing and Increase

November 2010

    We just did our second short sale. We really had no money in the bank because we used most of what we had to settle the debt with the bank. We borrowed on our primary home so at this point we owe $65,000 more on the house than it was worth.

Sept 2011

    God provides me with a new job. Then the Holy Spirit gives me wisdom to execute a strategy that wins us a deal that would become the largest customer in our region. Personally, our financial situation changes drastically as God showers us with Favor and Blessings.

Sept 2014

    In the last three years, God has allowed us to sell our home that we were upside down on and get rid of that debt. We moved to a new home He provided for us. We were able to buy at $100,000 less than market value. Our personal finances look nothing like they did four years prior and in the last two years we have given away over $120,000 dollars.

    It has truly been miraculous. To share the numbers of the income He provided and favor with my business and company would be hard to do without bragging on His goodness. The best way for me to describe it is a total 180-degree turnaround. On top of that, He just does fun things like have the insurance company pay for a new roof on our house, which cost $30,000. Also, He gave us the ability to complete our 2nd adoption without any debt!

Couple in their 30's

CHAPTER 9

Living from Abundance

Craig Hill wrote a parable of managing financial resource:[1]

Imagine a huge snowfield in the mountains with virtually an infinite supply of water. There were **three rivers** emanating from the snowfield. On the **First River**, lives a man whose experience of life is such that he never quite had enough water. So, what does he do with the water coming down the river? He builds a dam in the River, and collects all the water that he possibly can. No water is ever able to flow downstream for others to use. This man's view of water only includes that which is available to him in his lake. Therefore he must conserve water, and he must be very careful because there's never really enough coming down for him. No water is ever available to flow downstream for others.

If the flow of water is ever increased in his River, he will simply store it and increase the size of his lake. His perception is that the bigger lake he has, the more secure he is for the future.

Now, there's a **Second River** that flows down from the snowfield. The man who lives along this river has life experience that tells him there's usually plenty of water to meet his needs, so there is no need to build a dam in the River. However, there is never quite enough water to really meet all of his desires for water usage.

Thus, he uses all the water he can and lets a very small amount flow downstream for others to use. However, most of the water coming down the river is consumed by his ever-expanding needs/desires, so not much is left to flow downstream. This man's view of water is that there is more water available upstream, but

> *"Jesus approached life from a 'Third River' mentality."*

its volume and rate of flow is quite limited. Therefore, he uses all he can as it flows down through his property.

If the flow of water is increased in this river, this family will inevitably find new uses for the water. This man will build a swimming pool for his children. If water flow still increases, he will build a water park and install series of beautiful fountains on his property. No matter how much water comes down the river, there is never enough to really do everything he would like to do with the water.

Then there is a **Third River** and a man who also lives on this river. His experience of life is that there is so much water up there in that snowfield that no one can ever use all of the water coming down the river. As a result of his understanding, this man begins digging canals to outlying areas to help water the fields of others who don't live near a river. He empties as much water as he can out through the canals he has dug and there still seems to be more water flowing down the river than he can possibly use, so most of it still flows downstream for others to use.

Each year this man digs a few new canals out to his neighbors, who need water. In the next year, he has a plan for another three canals. Then the following year, he's hoping to dig five new canals that go even further from this river. It seems like no matter how many canals he digs, there's just more water that keeps coming down the river. As a matter fact, this man is thinking all the time about how he can hire some more men with bulldozers to dig the canals faster to get water out to all these other farms that are far from the river. This man's experience of life is that you just can't use up all that water coming down the river.

If the flow of water is increased in this river, the man living along this river will simply dig more canals to get more and more water out to help others.

On which river do you live?

God is the ultimate steward. He invests His resources into fertile ground—the surrendered heart.

JESUS KNEW SOMETHING OTHERS DID NOT KNOW

Jesus approached life from a "Third River" mentality. He walked around with the knowledge that, "I never have lack. If I come into a situation with lack, I'll dip into what I have inside of me and get rid of the lack. My Source in any situation is the God of Limitless Supply."[2] He showed us the abundant heart of the Father in every situation.

When the little boy brought his five loaves and two fishes to Jesus, did Jesus gobble them up and say, "I am giving you a lesson in poverty!"? Of course not! When Jesus fed the multitudes, did He give them each a mini-snack? Jesus didn't give the hungry crowd barely enough, He gave *more* than enough, "And they all ate and were satisfied. And [the disciples] took up twelve baskets full of the broken pieces left over" (Matthew 14:20). Bill Johnson says, "He is extravagant, but He isn't wasteful."

I have heard theologians try to spiritualize this story, "Jesus was showing that He had authority over the physical realm." Demonstrating His authority may have been a byproduct, but I don't think it was His purpose. There was a lack of food, so He dipped into the abundance of the Kingdom and blessed them with more than enough. He showed us the heart of the Father.

Our church got to experience this kind of miracle first hand. A group from our church was doing a church service for the homeless at a local mission. They brought three crockpots full of food, but didn't anticipate the size of the crowd that showed up. They definitely did not have enough salad, pie, or cookies either. They quickly told the volunteers and workers not to eat any of the food. They prayed over the food and blessed it. Here is the email I received from a girl in our church who was serving that day:

> So we started handing out food and I noticed the crockpots weren't emptying at all. They were like, getting fuller! We started piling the food on the plates and there was so much, people had trouble carrying it to the table. Spaghetti, meatballs, peaches, salad, pie and cookies! There were over 90 people all together. We went around to hand out cookies because there was so much extra. We ended up with extra pie, cookies, peaches and two full crockpots.

Not only was everyone fed, but people took food home with them! It's like the Bible!

Whether it was a shortage of food, someone sick or demonized, running out of wine at a wedding (an embarrassing social situation for the family), religious leaders trying to trick Him with questions, a crowd wanting to throw Him off of a cliff, a life-threatening storm, a funeral with a premature death, or forgiveness for those who crucified Him—Jesus was confident and secure. You never see a scripture that says, "And Jesus was worried," or "And Jesus was so stressed that He couldn't sleep," or "And Jesus had no idea what to do for this problem."

It's like Jesus had access to something other people did not. That "something" is *zoe*. God is not only inviting us into abundant life, but an abundant lifestyle.

"I HAVE COME THAT YOU MAY HAVE *ZOE*"

There is a kind of life that Jesus came to bring. I don't mean "life" in the sense of days and activities (that is the New Testament Greek word *bios*). The life Jesus brought was life in terms of quality and intensity—the same quality and intensity that Jesus Himself lived from. The New Testament Greek word that describes this "life" is *zoe*.[3] *Zoe* is the life that God has in Himself.[4] Jesus came so that we could have an abundance of this kind of life, "I came that they may have life (*zoe*) and have it abundantly" (John 10:10).

Dallas Willard talks about how there are different kinds of "life" between vegetables, animals, people, and God. If a ball of string were set in front of a head of cabbage, there would be no interaction because the kind of life in the cabbage cannot relate to a ball of string. If that ball of string were set before a kitten, there would be interaction because the kitten is full of the life of play. Set a poem in front of the kitten and there would be no response because animals are dead to the realm of poetry; however, a person can respond to poetry. Similarly, a relationship with God is necessary to respond to the abundant *zoe* Jesus came to bring.[5] If life is "the power to act and respond in certain kinds of relationships"[6]—Jesus came to bring us into an interactive relationship with God and access to the abundance of His Kingdom.

Jesus talked to Nicodemus about *zoe* in John 3. Jesus was trying to show Nicodemus how God's Spirit comes and moves in the life of an individual. People can see the results but they can't see what causes the results. This is abundant life: life lived from hidden sources that come into our life from God and His Kingdom. This abundant *zoe* is possible no matter where you are or what you may be doing.[7]

WHAT DOES *ZOE* FEEL LIKE?

When I was in seminary, I worked in an adult psychiatric ward. A small part of my job was to help restrain patients who were violent towards themselves or others. Each shift, one of the nurses would give an update on each patient to bring us up to speed on how a patient was responding to treatment, any behaviors we needed to be aware of, etc.

I remember one night, as my shift began, we received the report about a patient who had an exceptional violent outburst a few days before. I was off work for a few days, so this was the first I was hearing about the ordeal. His father was a Satanist (not joking) and this patient seemed to be in the family business. The day of the episode, he decided to pick his bed up from the ground with superhuman strength and throw it across the room. Some of the workers tried to stop him. He picked them up and threw them across the room too. That got my attention. I immediately began fasting and praying.

As my shift went on, I forgot about "The Thrower" until I heard the sound of crashing coming from his room. He was at it again. I went to the edge of the door only to see furniture flying across the room. He seemed to be in demonic-induced rage.

The hospital's training for these events was minimal. And I think I was absent the day that my seminary class covered how to stop coworkers from being thrown across the room. (This was during my "Pharisee days" where the Holy Spirit and authority over demons were more academic to me than reality.) Confrontation with violent people is not a strong area of spiritual passion or competence for me. However, it was my job to do something. I stood quivering in the doorway. And as his blackened eyes met mine, I knew I was about to be in my first physical confrontation since volunteering in the church nursery in high school (and those kids were tough!).

In the nursery, a simple "All right you guys, settle down, I'm serious!" works pretty well on three-year-olds who know you have access to their parents. But with the son of a satanic priest full of anti-psychotic drugs and demonic adrenaline, you feel a little less powerful.

Similar to my time with the three-year-olds, I prophesied to him, "If you don't settle down, I'm going to have to escort you to the 'time out' room." (That's actually what we called it. It sounds nicer than the "locked, isolated room with the 5-point leather restraints.").

Something unexpected happened. "The Thrower" suddenly looked up at me with fear in his eyes. I was shocked. I began to relish the thoughts about how much spiritual power I must be carrying that my mere presence could calm the storm raging inside of him.

Then I looked behind me. There was "Big Rick." He was a football player at a local college. He was 6'8" and weighed around 320 pounds, with the majority of that being muscle. If Hercules had married Xena the Warrior Princess, Big Rick would be their offspring. Big Rick did not say a word; his physique did the talking. I could tell he was hoping for a physical confrontation. He scored high on "fights" and "confrontations" on the spiritual passion test and he had great competence.

Something unexpected changed in me at that moment. I started making bold declarations, "Yeah, you had better settle down…" I was a different person because Big Rick was with me. My quivering turned to confidence and courage. My buckling knees turned to boldness. Fear and anxiety fled like rats from a sinking ship.

Why? Because Big Rick was with me. His giant muscles and grimacing face comforted me. Being in a room with a violent demoniac was a perfectly safe place to be. If I knew Big Rick was with me 24/7, I would have a different approach to life and dangerous situations.

But I don't need Big Rick with me. [8]

I have the One who said, "I will be with you always" (Matthew 28:20). "I will never fail you. I will never abandon you" (Hebrews 13:5 NLT). Listen to this same verse in the Amplified Bible:

> …for He [God] Himself has said, I will not in any way fail you nor give you up nor leave you without support. [I will] not, [I will] not, [I will] not in any degree leave you helpless nor forsake nor let [you] down (relax My hold on you)! [Assuredly not!]

Here's the truth: **when you have God, you have everything.** God has ALL the provisions—and you have God. Prosperity is not what you have; it's Who you have. You don't feel better about yourself because of your bank account or possessions. You are confident because of Who is with you— Abundant Life Himself. If you've received the gift of Christ, you have no reason to think or act as if you lack anything.

Some have pointed out that when John 10:10 talks about "abundant life" it is not talking about money. I agree. It is promising something *much* bigger. A believer can now interact with Christ and His Kingdom and pull the strength, wisdom, healing, peace, provision, power, love—whatever you need to bring into that situation. We can't limit this verse merely to financial provision.

Author Stephen DeSilva captures this "abundance" thinking:

> ...the central message of prosperity [is this]: In the Kingdom, there is always enough because God is without limit and Christ has declared us worthy to receive all that is His as His sons and daughters. It is this precious relationship with Him that determines our worth and what we deserve. [9]

"In the Kingdom, there is always enough."

GOD HAS A PLAN FOR YOUR LIFE, SO DOES THE DEVIL

If you listen to some preachers, you'd think the only way to grow is to have something horrible happen in your life. They talk about the valleys, write worship songs about the valleys, and even develop programs to help people get into a valley. "Do you need a valley? We can help!" Religion often fixates on one truth while ignoring another. Many have created a picture of the Christian life that says, "I have to go through the valley to get to where I want to go"—that is a truth. We can grow from valleys and trials. But God wants us to learn from the mountaintops too!

Thank God the verse does not end at, "The thief comes only to steal and kill and destroy" (John 10:10). John goes on to say, "I came that they may have life and have it abundantly" (John 10:10). "That they may have" is a phrase in the Greek that means "to have and to continually possess."

"Abundantly" means "to be above, beyond what is regular, extraordinary, or even exceeding. This is not just abundance; it is super-abundance." [10] Here is Rick Renner's "expanded interpretive translation" of the second part of John 10:10:

> ...But I came that they might have, keep, and constantly retain a vitality, gusto, vigor, and zest for living that springs up from deep down inside. I came that they might embrace this unrivaled, unequaled, matchless, incomparable, richly loaded and overflowing life to the ultimate maximum! [11]

And [Jesus] left them, got into the boat again, and went to the other side. Now they had forgotten to bring bread, and they had only one loaf with them in the boat. And He cautioned them, saying, "Watch out; beware of the leaven of the Pharisees and the leaven of Herod." And they began discussing with one another the fact that they had no bread. And Jesus, aware of this, said to them, "Why are you discussing the fact that you have no bread? Do you not yet perceive or understand? Are your hearts hardened? Having eyes do you not see, and having ears do you not hear? And do you not remember? When I broke the five loaves for the five thousand, how many baskets full of broken pieces did you take up?" They said to Him, "Twelve." "And the seven for the four thousand, how many baskets full of broken pieces did you take up?" And they said to Him, "Seven." And He said to them, "Do you not yet understand?" (Mark 8:13-21).

By the time we get to this story, Jesus already performed two miracles of multiplying food: He fed 5000 with five loaves and two fish and had twelve baskets full of leftovers (Mark 6:30-44); and He fed 4000 with seven loaves and a few small fish and had seven baskets full of leftovers (Mark 8:1-10). And *now* the disciples are afraid of not having enough lunch!

Jesus gives His disciples a mini-sermon about two leavens. Bill Johnson notes that the two leavens represent two different influences on the mind; both of these leavens are motivated by the fear of man/concern over what people will think about what we say or do.[12] The leaven of the Pharisees is where God is present in theory, but absent in our experience or practice. The concept of God is central, but the experience of God is removed. The leaven of Herod represents that "political spirit" where we use popular opinion, persuasion, control, and manipulation to get our will done. God exists, we just exclude Him entirely. Each of these "leavens" is trying to shape our view of reality. Jesus lived from a different reality. He fed more people when He started with less and had more leftover.

Jesus begins with this question, "Why are you discussing the fact that you have no bread?" (Mark 8:17). In other words, "Why does your thought life begin with what you lack?" **Once you have been exposed to the Kingdom**

it is no longer acceptable to start with what you don't have. When you have seen God do a miracle, you have a legal precedent and you bring this history to your new situation. Any thought that begins with what we don't have must be repented of.

"Jesus was trying to teach them to see through the miracle they had just experienced."

When I was getting ready to graduate from seminary, we still owed $4000 that school loans didn't cover. I would not be able to graduate without paying this off, and we did not have the money. I was pretty scared and had never seen God provide supernaturally like this before. Mary and I got on our knees on a Sunday night and took the need to Him. It is pretty easy to pray when you are at the end of your resources. As much as we would have wanted to, we felt like we were not supposed to share the need with anyone.

Three days later, we got a check in the mail for $1000 from friend of the family I hadn't talked to in over five years. Thursday we got a check for $2000 from a distant relative I hadn't talked to in over ten years and another for $1080 from a close family member. We received $4080 in four days without sharing the need with anyone but the Lord. Yea God!

However, I remember the next time we had a financial need I was just as scared as the first time I needed the miracle. The heat of adversity caused the leaven of the Pharisees to rise in my life. I didn't forget about the other miracle; I just didn't let it feed my heart so that I saw differently. God seemed more like a theory in that moment.

Jesus was trying to teach His disciples to see through the miracle they had just experienced. It is like those previous miracles had nutrients in them to strengthen them for the next situation. Miracles are a tutor to teach us how to see. Why couldn't they see? They had a hard heart because they didn't consider the previous miracles (Mark 6:52).

Jesus asks three questions to help them learn: "Do you not see? Do you not hear? Do you not remember?" Bill Johnson points out that we can't always see what God is doing. There are many times we are not hearing what He is saying. But we can remember. If we get our eyes off of the problem long enough, we can remember. And remembering will activate our capacity to hear which will activate our capacity to see. We have to develop our thinking around our history with God.

If you can't see, hear, or remember stories of provision in your own life, steal someone else's testimony to ponder. Psalm 119:111, "Your testimonies are my heritage forever…" Feed yourself on the stories of God working in other people's lives, and those will become part of your arsenal. (You can start with some of the "Heaven Invading" testimonies before each chapter in this book!)

POVERTY THINKING VS. *ZOE* THINKING

At the heart of "*zoe* thinking" is the understanding that "there is always enough." Not only that—it goes deeper. It is the declaration and belief that "there is always enough *for me*." You realize you are rich with or without money because you have Christ. You have access to the very things He had access to, "For all things are yours…and you are Christ's, and Christ is God's" (1 Corinthians 3:21-23). Being desperate for things we already have access to is choosing to live in a state of unbelief.

"When you live in the realm of abundance, you realize Who and what you have access to."

If the only time I answer my kid's requests is if they are begging and on the verge of disaster, then I am not a good father:

"Dad, the doctor said if we don't eat soon, we will die. Will you please feed me now?"

"Kids, that's what I've been waiting for. I heard your stomachs growling, but I didn't think you wanted it bad enough. I like it when my kids are desperate—it really keeps you humble."

What's the difference between desperation and hunger? Desperation is a focus on the awareness of lack. Hunger realizes the fridge is full and I am going to get off the couch and go get some food. When you live in the realm of abundance, you realize Who and what you have access to. The essence of a covenant is "I will be your God and you will be My people. I will be in your midst. All of Me for all of you."

To help clarify what living from abundance looks like, let's contrast

132

"poverty thinking" with "*zoe* thinking." It goes beyond a "glass is half empty" versus a "glass is half full" mentality because *zoe* thinking is rooted in the reality of Who God is and Who He has promised to be for you.

- Poverty thinking says, "If it is going to be, it is up to me." *Zoe* thinking says, "The Lord is my Shepherd. There is nothing I lack" (Psalm 23:1 HCSB).
- Poverty thinking says, "I am a victim. Things just happen to me. I was born into the wrong family. If only I had been..." *Zoe* thinking says, "I am an overcomer—that means I am going to have some things to overcome which will only strengthen me and write my history with God."
- Poverty looks at a situation in terms of what is humanly possible, "I can't see how we are going to ever get out of debt." *Zoe* thinking looks to partner with the God of the impossible. The anthem is, "We cut off the giant's head, we eat giants for our bread."[13] I see things differently; the impossible looks logical.
- Poverty thinking gets jealous when someone else gets blessed or has a testimony. *Zoe* thinking rejoices at another story of Dad's goodness and celebrates their victory as if it were your own.
- Poverty thinking believes, "I will never get my break." *Zoe* thinking knows you have the attention and favor of the God of the universe, and when the time comes for you to be promoted, He will open doors that no man can shut. Until then, you serve and work as if you were working for the Lord.
- Poverty thinking says, "If I just had more money" or "If I just had this one more thing/spouse/job...then I would be happy." *Zoe* thinking is content with what God has provided. Stephen DeSilva describes it this way: "Even as you passionately run after the things God has put on your heart, you do so from a place of rest and gratitude, knowing that your source of happiness is not achievement but His abiding presence."[14]
- Poverty thinking approaches a situation full of worry, anxiety, greed, panic, and feeling out of control. *Zoe* thinking is full of peace, relaxation, trust, joy, and a sense of dominion.
- Poverty thinking learns to see life through the lens of their disappointments and valleys. *Zoe* thinking grows through trials and valleys, but learns to see from the mountaintops as well.

When you renew your mind from poverty thinking to *zoe* thinking, the way you see reality changes. *Zoe* thinking gives you "perspectacles" that will anchor you in the truth of Who is in you and with you, regardless of circumstances.

The abundant life that Jesus came to bring is not so you can get rich, but so you can develop a prosperous soul and can live from the resources of the Kingdom in every situation. In doing this, you never meet a situation in your own strength, but in the strength of Christ.

LIVING ON THE THIRD RIVER

Let's go back to Craig Hill's parable of the three rivers. We know that God has an infinite supply of resources, right? If this is true, then why is it that churches and Kingdom ministries seemed to have a limited supply of resources and scarcity? Is God stingy with His people? No. How does resource get from God's supply to these ministries? Primarily through people. Craig Hill notes:

Each Christian is like a pipeline through which God desires to flow financial resource into the Kingdom. However, many of the pipelines are extremely clogged and leaky. Most of what God puts down the pipe never makes it out the other end.[15]

If you are the person in the snowfield who decides how much water to release into each river, which river would you tend to put most of the water down? Craig Hill has brilliant insight here:

I'd put most of the water down river number three. How much are you going to release into river number one? I would probably put enough down this river to meet the need of that man who lives down there because I love him, and want him to be taken care of. However, there's no use for that water making a large lake on his property. It just becomes stagnant, like a Dead Sea. So, I'd just put enough water down there for that family to use. [And that stagnant water would become dangerous for him to consume anyway.]

How much water would you put in the second river? I

would probably send only enough water to meet the need of the people who live along that river. There is no point in sending huge quantities of water down this river, as it will be improperly used. The majority of water will of course be sent down the third river, so that it will be utilized to bring the most benefit to the greatest number of people.[16]

So many Christians are "sowing seeds," making "confessions of faith," and believing God for "the wealth of the wicked to be transferred to the righteous" while they are still living on the first and second rivers. After reading Craig's parable, do you see how it would be irresponsible of God to have someone "win the Jesus lotto" and bless them with financial prosperity when it would only feed first and second river lifestyles? I have found in my own life that it is easier to give money away or pray than to steward it. In the parable of the ten minas, we see that faithfulness gets rewarded with more resources to steward for the Master (Luke 19:11-27).

Craig concludes with this prophetic insight:

In reality, whatever water is flowing down your river right now is probably about the amount that God finds you faithful to manage. If you desire to manage a greater portion of God's resources as a steward, this will require that you allow God to change you significantly on the inside. You will first need to learn to be faithful over what you have been given to manage now. The Lord can then bring about the necessary change in your thinking and perceptions of life to be able to understand how to manage greater amounts of resources in His Kingdom.

When I have learned how to live along the third river with the resources I now have, I qualify myself to receive more of God's resources to channel into His Kingdom. The faster I can learn to build canals and channel resources into the Kingdom, the faster I qualify myself to handle more resources. I believe that the Lord is simply looking for people with a credible track record, not people who are merely full of good intentions for the future. "When I have more money, I will give thus and such," they say, as they continue to mismanage what they have now. For many of us, this is a major paradigm shift that will have to take place now in order to qualify us for the plan God has for us for the future.[17]

WHAT RIVER ARE YOU CURRENTLY LIVING ON?

Here's a quick test:

- People who live on the **1ˢᵗ and 2ⁿᵈ Rivers** spend first and give and invest what's left. People who live on the **3ʳᵈ River** give and invest first, and spend what's left.
- People who live on the **1ˢᵗ and 2ⁿᵈ Rivers** are excited when they get extra money so they can spend it on themselves. People on the **3ʳᵈ River** are excited to be able to give more.
- People on the **1ˢᵗ and 2ⁿᵈ Rivers** measure prosperity by how much money or how nice of a house or possessions they have. People on the **3ʳᵈ River** measure prosperity by how much of a blessing are they to someone else.
- People on the **1ˢᵗ and 2ⁿᵈ Rivers** set goals for income. **Third River** people set goals for giving and investing.
- People on the **1ˢᵗ and 2ⁿᵈ Rivers** give to get. **Third River** people give to get so they can give away even more.

When you get to where the priority of your finances isn't about you, but to bless someone else, then God will assume the liability of taking care of you. And when God takes care of you, He will take care of you better than you would ever take care of yourself.

What river are you currently living on?

What river do you desire to live along?

INNER ACTION

1. Read these verses and allow John's vision to fill your thoughts:

Then the angel showed me the river of the water of life, as clear as crystal, flowing from the throne of God and of the Lamb down the middle of the great street of the city. On each side of the river stood the tree of life, bearing twelve crops of fruit, yielding its fruit every month. And the leaves of the tree are for the healing of the nations. No longer will there be any curse. The throne of God and of the Lamb will be in the city, and His servants will serve Him. They will see His face, and His name will be on their foreheads. There will be no more night. They will not need the light of a lamp or the light of the sun, for the Lord God will give them light. And they will reign forever and ever (Revelation 22:1-5 NIV).

2. Stephen DeSilva gives this tool for training our thinking away from a paradigm of lack to a paradigm of plenty:

The river of God is a picture of abundant life, supernatural provision and prosperity. Everything good you will ever need or desire can be found in it. It runs through the middle of the street, giving everyone full access to it. All you need to do is learn how to get into the flow.

Now, engage your imagination further by activating your body. Stand up and imagine you are standing in the river, facing downstream, away from the Throne. Behind you, God is placing good things into the river for you. Yet, because of your position, you remain a spectator, watching good things float past you, just out of reach. Try to envision what some of those good things might be. Speak this prayer aloud:

Father God, I am standing in the crystal river of heaven that flows from Your Throne. You fill this river with good things, but because I am facing downstream, good things flow away from me. They are just beyond my reach, too hard to catch.

Lord Jesus, I want to turn. I want to see Your Throne. I want to see Your provision. I turn around, in Jesus' name. [Physically turn and face the opposite direction.]

Thank You, God, that I am facing upstream. I can envision the Throne of God and the Lamb. Good things are coming to me. The good things are everywhere. There's more than I can contain. There is abundance here for everyone. In Jesus' name, Amen.

3.   Imagine what it looks, sounds, smells, tastes, and feels like to stand in the flow of this river's immeasurable abundance. There is no limitation, no lack. God places good things in this river for you and everyone connected to you. These good things flow toward you and they're easy to catch. The new position you now occupy creates a new paradigm of expectancy. Facing the Source of abundance drives away the fear, insecurity, and powerlessness you previously felt as you watched good things pass you by. From this new view, you expect good things. You expect that every need will be met at the right time. You expect that nothing will be impossible. You know that everything in your Father's Kingdom is yours.[18]

Additional Resources

Money and the Prosperous Soul by Stephen DeSilva
Living on the Third River by Craig Hill

Endnotes

1. Craig Hill, *Living on the Third River* (Littleton, CO: Family Foundations International, 2002), 1-3. Used with author's permission.

2. Eric Johnson shared an amazing message at the 2010 Bethel Church Fall Leaders' Advance in Redding, CA that influenced my thinking on this subject.

3. When John uses "life" or "eternal life" it is similar to the way Matthew, Mark and Luke use the "Kingdom of God." Gordon D. Fee, *The Disease of the Health and Wealth Gospels* (A Regent College Reprint, 1996), 7. A technical definition of *zoe* in John is "the life of the kingdom era [now] available to those living in the present through faith in Christ" in Craig S. Keener, *The Gospel of John: A Commentary Volume 1* (Peabody, MA: Hendrickson, 2003), 329.

4. "Zoe" is defined as "…life in the absolute sense, life as God has it, that which the Father has in Himself , and which He gave to the Incarnate Son to have in Himself…" in W.E. Vine, *An Expository Dictionary of New Testament Words* (Fleming, CO; Old Tappan, 1966), 336 cited in Malcolm Smith, *Spiritual Burnout* (Tulsa, OK: Pillar Books, 1995), 56

5. Cited in Midwest District Blog entry "Starting Large" at http://mwcma. wordpress.com/tag/dallas-willard/ entered February 21, 2013 accessed August 28, 2014.

6. Ibid.

7. Dallas Willard, "Your Place in This World" accessed from http://www.dwillard. org/articles/artview.asp?artID=109 on August 28, 2014. It was published in 2005 by LifeWay Christian Resources in the Holman CSB *Graduate's Bible*, this was Dr. Willard's commencement address at Greenville College in May 2004. Transcribed and edited by Steve Bond of Holman Bible Publishers.

8. The story of "Big Rick" is completely mine and true, but I was reminded of it based on a story that John Ortberg told in *If You Want to Walk on the Water, You've Got to Get Out of the Boat* (Grand Rapids: Zondervan, 2001), 193-194. The style of my story as well as the application were inspired by Ortberg's story.

9. Stephen DeSilva, *Money and the Prosperous Soul* (Grand Rapids: Chosen, 2010), 132.

10. Rick Renner, *Sparkling Gems From the Greek* (Tulsa, OK: Teach All Nations, 2003), 548.

11. Ibid.

12. This section was inspired by the teaching of Bill Johnson in his message "The Supernatural Power of a Renewed Mind Part 4: Eyes of a Tender Heart." I heard Bill teach on this passage again in May 2014 at the Hem of His Garment Healing School in Redding, CA. Most of this section is from notes I took on these messages. Used with permission.

13. Lyrics from "You're An Army" by Rick Pino from the album *Songs For An End Time Army* (Fire Rain Music, 2009).

14. DeSilva, 70.

15. Hill, 44.

16. Ibid., 45.

17. Ibid., 46.

18. DeSilva, 157-158. Used with author's permission.

Conclusion

After I taught eighteen weeks in a row on finances at our church (the basis for this book series), someone asked me, "What is your big takeaway?" Without hesitation I replied, "God really does love me, and I can trust Him with everything."

What if *everything* about money is designed to teach you how to trust God? Or even better, just how trustworthy God really is?

There is only one way to live for God: in wonder. That is part of what it means to be childlike; with kids, everything is an adventure. You live in this sense of wonder, "Dad, You are so big, so brilliant, so good, so sneaky... anything is possible!"

As you go through your days, your attitude is, "I wonder what God is going to do today. I wonder what is going to happen in this situation." You don't have time to be intimidated by the enemy; you are too fascinated by Jesus. "I wonder how God sees this situation? I wonder what He wants to do in me?"

Through each situation, you live in dependency and wonder. You discover the depth and width and length of God's love for you. It is no longer theory; He is showing you who He really is by experience.

Graham Cooke says, "Only God has abundance; the enemy has a budget." In the last few years, has God somehow mysteriously gone broke? If God is the only One who has abundance and He owns it all; if He has not changed, then why have some stopped tithing and giving?

When we start to withhold our finances and get fearful, we take our lives back from God. That won't work because you are in charge now and, on your own, you are in a recession. The sensible thing to do is to figure out ways to increase your giving. God's ways are not the world's ways. We don't look to the world or to our bank account for security and peace.

When difficult times come, you need to put yourself even more firmly in the hands of God. When money is tight, that is the time for relentless trust. So, what if you made trusting the Lord the most enjoyable thing ever?

Let's say that you get a bill that you don't know how you are going to pay; or you decide to get out of debt and suddenly you lose your job. You have a friend who knows your situation and asks, "What are you going to do?"

"I'm trusting the Lord, of course!"

"What about your finances?" they probe further.

"They are a little bit sticky right now, but I am trusting the Lord. I just increased my giving, because I am not dumb. I believe the Bible. That is why I am not worried. I am planning on having an adventure. I can't wait to see what God is going to be for me. I put my life in His hands. I put my finances in His hands. I am just going to have fun with the whole thing."[1]

God is waiting to have some fresh encounters with you. Every trial is an opportunity for an upgrade in your relationship with Him. God can now be something for you that He couldn't be before. Testing times are the doorway into the heart of God.

The Holy Spirit will guide you into all truth (John 16:13), not just tell you truth. This means that you will be put in the exact opposite circumstance of the truth He is teaching you by experience. How will you learn peace? Your circumstances will be the exact opposite of peaceful. Your only peace will come from Him. You can feast on His reality and live in His atmosphere.

If trusting God with your finances is not a delight, then you have an invitation to an upgrade of your walk with Him. And if you trust God for that which is least (money), then you can be trusted with true riches.

Dream for a moment:

- What could your life look like if for the next six months you went on an all-out adventure with God by living in wonder and making trust a delight?
- What kind of peace would you experience?
- What kind of miracles could you see?
- How much of a blessing could you be?

- What seeds would you sow in the Spirit and the natural for your future generations?
- What influence could you have in your sphere?
- What would it be like to leave an inheritance for your children's children's children?

PART 2

Now that you have learned "The Foundation For Supernatural Finances" from this book, I encourage you to read the sequel, *How Heaven Invades Your Finances Book 2: Revolutionize Your Living, Giving & Receiving.*

Since giving is not something you do in order to make God bless you, how does giving fit into the true Gospel message—that God blesses you because Christ made us righteous, not because of our performance? Here are some of the topics we'll explore:

- What Must I Do to Receive God's Blessings?
- Crucial Moments
- A Plan for Prosperity
- How to Get Back in the Black
- Giving Under Grace
- How Much Should I Give?
- Need, Greed or Seed?
- Why, Where, and When to Give
- The Key to Everything

Endnotes

1. That scenario was adapted from one in a message by Graham Cooke, "The Church Has Left The Building" Disc One. Available at www.BrilliantPerspectives.com.

ABOUT THE AUTHOR

Jim Baker and Mary, his wife of 20+ years, are the senior pastors of Zion Christian Fellowship in Powell, Ohio. The church is marked by worship, a strong presence of God, healings, miracles, several dead raisings and a passion for personal and regional transformation. You can access his additional resources at BakersEquip.ecwid.com, which includes teachings on Finances, Healing, and Identity. Here is more about Jim in his own words:

My clan: Mary, the woman of my dreams, is a relentless encourager, balance-bringer, and partner in ministry. I have three amazing boys who love the Lord and have inherited my love for superhero movies. I can still take them in wrestling, but it's getting close.

Life mission: To transform and equip people to supernaturally demonstrate God's Kingdom in their sphere of influence.

Things I am gifted at: Remembering the words to 80's TV theme songs, break dancing, saying the books of the Bible faster than any other human.

Things I'm **not** *gifted at:* Anything mechanical, directions, and singing (this is the short list).

My other dream job: Being a Ninja (minus the killing part, I guess that just leaves wearing the black pajama outfit).

Hobbies: Movies, cars (especially Audi, Nissan GTR's, Corvettes, and American muscle), futile attempts to look like the guy on the Bowflex commercial, reading, time with my kids, evenings with my wife, high-speed go-kart racing, and table tennis (you can't call it ping-pong if you sweat).

Authors of influence: Bill Johnson, Dallas Willard, Andrew Wommack, Craig Hill, Malcolm Smith, John Ortberg, Gordon Fee, Craig Keener, John Wimber, Dave Ramsey.

Things that make my heart beat fast: Revival, my wife, watching my family grow in their spiritual journey, life in the Kingdom of God, the potential of the emerging generation, divine healing, world missions, seeing a life transformed, seeing an unsaved friend take a step forward on their spiritual journey, serving the P.O.W.S. (Poor, Orphans, Widows, Single Parents), and marketplace ministry.

Places I've paid tuition: University of Michigan (B.A. Psychology), Assemblies of God Theological Seminary (M.A. Counseling, M.Div.).

Made in the USA
Coppell, TX
08 May 2021